I0568128

# The
# Journal

# The Journal

## An Unexpected Encounter with Jesus

Nancy Kurkowski & Jimmy Decker

invite
PRESS

Plano, Texas

*For Dad, who always had a story for us.*
*I love you.*
*—Nancy*


*To my son, Max. I pray I share the gospel story with you*
*just as Nancy's dad did for her.*
*—Jimmy*

# Introduction to the Story and Guide for Reading

The story of Salome and Mariam is a work of fiction but is based on biblical accounts of Jesus from all four Gospels. It was inspired by an Ash Wednesday sermon preached several years ago in Penney Farms, Florida, by my father, Rev. David L. Allen. My father could always tell a story that put the listener in the time and place of his characters. This story is intended to do the same, to help internalize the fact that Jesus was a real man who would have taken a similar journey to Jerusalem the week before his death. He would have known what was coming, and he would have had these types of conversations with his followers as they walked along. My father passed along to me an intimate relationship with Jesus, and we hope that this story helps to do the same for you.

This book contains both a story in the form of a personal journal and an accompanying devotional. You can read the story straight through and do the devotional in your own time, or you can choose to read the daily sections of the devotional that complement certain events within the story. No matter which way you choose to read, we hope that this experience leaves you feeling encouraged, faithful, and refreshed.

Nancy Kurkowski

# The Journal

## 1:Tuesday Afternoon

"**J**esus of Nazareth is walking with us," my husband Mattathias says excitedly as he ducks through the door. We are preparing for the walk to Jerusalem that Mattathias takes almost every year. This year, I can go along, because he is allowing our twelve-year-old son, Honi, to come also. It's common for many of the people from the villages surrounding the Sea of Galilee to walk together to Jerusalem to celebrate the Feast of Unleavened Bread at the temple. The journey will be a walk of about three days, and we will pick up more and more people as we walk along. Mattathias is excited, because this Jesus that he is speaking of is an amazing man who has recently made his home here in Capernaum not far from our house. He teaches things that no one has heard before, and he has healed many people. He has a small group of close friends who are plain people like we are. They seem to have left their homes to follow him and learn from him.

Jesus himself is a craftsman, a worker in stone and wood. Before he came to Capernaum, he worked with his father and brothers in many of the nearby towns. Lately, though, he and his disciples spend their time teaching in and around Galilee, down in Judea, and even in Samaria. He always has time to listen to those who come to him with their problems. If he is walking with us, the trip will be even more exciting.

We need to pack lightly, but I've pulled together a pack for each of us to carry containing a pallet to sleep on, a change of clothes for when we get to the city, an extra pair of sandals, and a few eating utensils. We will take some food, but much of the food that we need we will buy in the villages along the way. I can't help being a little nervous about what I'll wear in Jerusalem, especially in the temple. It's been many years since I've been there, and I want to fit in. We will be staying with my cousin Mariam and her husband, Yohanan. They have a nice house and are more sophisticated than we are. I love Mariam. I don't think she'll intentionally make me feel self-conscious, but I still worry that I will seem simple compared to her. Of course, Honi is excited, because this will be his first trip outside of Galilee, and he will get to meet my cousin's son, John Mark, who is also twelve years old.

Mattathias is a laborer and works in the fields and orchards surrounding Capernaum. Luckily, it is not harvest time, and the landowner is a pious man who always encourages Mattathias to make this journey. He says that we will be able to stay with Mariam and Yohanan for a few extra days. I know that he always looks forward to this time of year.

"Everything seems ready," Mattathias yawns. "We should go to bed early." But then he continues talking about how he hopes to be able to have a conversation with Jesus. I know he has been wondering about some of Jesus' teachings. We all have. The rumor is that John, whom everyone calls "the Baptizer," claimed that he was not worthy to baptize Jesus. But he did, and people say that everyone saw the Spirit of God descend onto Jesus when John baptized him in the Jordan River. After that, many of John's disciples started following Jesus. John insists that Jesus is the one he has been preaching about, the one in whom God's Spirit will dwell and who will finally bring God's kingdom to us!

These days, Jesus is always surrounded by crowds, and more and more people seek him out every day. He knows so much about Scripture, and he says such unusual things about what God's kingdom will be like. Just like John, Jesus talks about repentance and the fact that we need to turn around and change our spiritual direction. I think he means that we are all focused on our own lives and our own desires but that we are supposed to be focused on God's plan for the world. One of my friends is married to our rabbi, and she says that her husband feels a little intimidated by Jesus, because he talks like he knows something that no one else knows. He doesn't just read the Scriptures and repeat the teachings that we have all heard before. Jesus is a charismatic man, that's for sure. But he is still humble and kind, as far as I can see. I know that if we have the chance to get near him, he will be easy to talk with.

## 2:Tuesday Evening

Mattathias, Honi, and I live in a two-room house which was added onto his parents' house when we were married. It is made of mud bricks and has an earthen floor, several small windows, and a raised platform at one end of the front room where we can sit and where we roll out our sleeping mats at night. The back room is very small, and I use it to store food in clay jars, to hang dried herbs, and to keep the few utensils that we own. It is a modest house, but we are fortunate to sit adjacent to the open courtyard which joins us to Mattathias' family's home. The courtyard is partially covered by an awning made of animal skins and is also where our fire pit is located. We share some simple stone implements for grinding grain and pressing olives and a cistern for collecting the rain that falls. Like most families, we even have our own small latrine and a simple mikveh which is hidden behind a screen of reeds for privacy. The mikveh is where my family bathes both for hygiene and for ritual cleansing.

Thankfully, I am happy living here next to Mattathias' parents and his younger brother's family. We get along well enough. We often share cooking duties, and it's fun to watch the children play. They love to draw squares in the sand and play a jumping game which involves moving pebbles around. My father-in-law has made some wooden spinning toys that keep them occupied for longer than you'd expect. Most days, we sit around the fire pit and enjoy our evening meal together. It is a simple but blessed life.

The rustling in the house finally stops, everyone settles down, and sleep comes easily. Tomorrow will be the beginning of a special adventure.

## 3: Wednesday Morning

I wake up to a beautiful spring morning with the sun just beginning to appear, and I go out into the courtyard. I climb up the ladder to the flat roof where I usually hang our clothes to dry and where we sleep when it is too hot to sleep inside. I love to come up here to pray and to have a few minutes of peace before the day's chores begin. Right now, though, I can hear a group of people starting to gather by the synagogue, so I hurry back down to wake up Mattathias and Honi. The synagogue is in the center of the village next to the well, and after we gather up our supplies, the three of us hurry there to join the other travelers.

Sure enough, Jesus and his disciples are there in the middle of the crowd. Of course, I've seen him around the village, and I have heard him teach several times, but he is always surrounded by people. We've spoken only a few times, but there is one encounter that especially moved me. It was several months ago. I had recently lost my mother, and I missed her dearly. I was sitting in my garden, quietly grieving. Although my mother-in-law and I share a small garden where we grow onions, beans, peppers, and garlic, I also have my own little patch where I grow herbs like dill and mint. I didn't think anyone would notice me there, and of course, it is unusual for a man to speak to an unaccompanied woman anyway. I was crying when Jesus walked by and was surprised when he stopped. I noticed that he also had tears in his eyes. "You won't be separated forever," he said quietly, "and you are not alone in your pain." He was looking at me like he genuinely cared about my sorrow, and I've always had the strangest feeling that he knew exactly what I had been crying about. I didn't know how to respond. He just smiled and moved on. But I felt something. Comfort, maybe? I have never forgotten that. I don't understand everything that Jesus teaches, but I know that he's a good man who seems to be able to see into your soul. He treats everyone as if they are special to him. Mattathias is as fascinated as I am with the man.

Eager for the journey to begin, the children are running around with pent-up energy. We gather with our friends, and soon the crowd starts to move together out of town. For this first part of our journey, we'll walk along the water and down the west side of the Sea of Galilee. We will stay close to the water's edge where the ground is flat and the path is well trodden. There are many villages up in the hills to the west of the Sea of Galilee. I know that many people from those villages will also be walking to Jerusalem over the next few days, and some of them will join us. The sun is warm now and the sky is clear. The sea beside our path is often unpredictable, but today it's calm. Mattathias told me that he heard about one time when Jesus was out in a boat with his disciples. A sudden storm came up and almost capsized their boat. But Jesus told the water to quiet, and it did. Instantly! And I've heard people talk about another time when Jesus actually walked right on top of the water. In our village, many people have stories like that about the amazing things Jesus has done. My brother swears that he was present when Jesus cured a young girl who had been declared dead. And I have several friends who were there when he fed thousands of people from just a few fish and loaves of bread. We all wonder about the wisdom that this man possesses, because there is definitely something powerful, yet kind, about his manner. No one has met anyone like him before. More and more people are saying that the Baptizer might be right and that Jesus might be the Messiah we have been waiting for.

## 4: Wednesday Afternoon

I am enjoying the gentle breeze, and so far the walk is fairly easy. There are fishing boats off to our left, and a few boats have been pulled up onto the shore. Several fishermen are standing in the water working on their nets. Since some of Jesus' closest disciples are also fishermen, I can hear them calling out good-natured greetings to their friends out in the water. A lovely field of grass flanks the lake where the wildflowers are beginning to bloom in bright colors. Happily, the sky is clear, and I can see the birds enjoying their view of us from up there.

On our right, I can see gentle hills where the olive groves are green and beautiful. The rainy season has come to an end, but everything is still fresh and alive. There is a grape vineyard in the distance, and I know that, over the next day or so, we will pass fields of barley and wheat, as well as lush orchards where pomegranates, figs, and oranges will soon grow.

I can feel the responsibilities of my daily routine slipping away. Most of us have grown up together, so we visit, and even sing, as we walk along. Honi is running ahead with some friends, and because Mattathias is anxious to hear what Jesus is saying, he also strides ahead. I am so grateful for my life, for my son, and for a husband who treats me well. I love the fact that my father taught me the Scriptures, even though I couldn't go to school at the synagogue like my brothers. Mostly right now, I am excited to be making this journey, especially with Jesus here. It feels special.

As I walk, I remember the lessons that my father taught me and my brothers about the expected Messiah. For many generations, our people have believed that a savior Messiah would come to inaugurate the kingdom of God on earth. He will bring God's kingdom here to us and transform the world back into what God intended it to be. This kingdom will be a world in which there is no sickness or sadness or injustice, and where death will be conquered forever. My father said that some people believe that even the dead will be resurrected and that we will all live in peace. God will be our king. What a world that would be!

Could Jesus be that savior? He is wonderful in his teaching, and many of the things that he says are similar to what my father used to talk about. But he is certainly not in a position of power, and I don't see how he could usher in God's kingdom. He doesn't seem to have many powerful friends. Also, he spends a great deal of time teaching about how God requires us to actively participate in bringing that kingdom to earth by practicing justice and forgiveness. He says that we must all serve one another, and above all else love one another, if we want to be called children of God. He says that God's kingdom is near.

I see injustice and sadness all around me, though. When my mother was sick, I couldn't understand why God would allow such a lovely person to suffer. I still don't understand. But my heart is warmed when I listen to Jesus, when I hear that God is with us in our suffering, and that one day everything will be made right again. When Jesus speaks like this, I am filled with hope for that long-awaited kingdom. I just don't understand how it is actually going to happen. Will Jesus do something to make it happen?

A group of men, and also a few women, surround Jesus and talk with him as we walk. Jesus actually has some women that he counts as disciples! He teaches that we are all equal. Women and men, even servants and their masters, are all equal in God's kingdom. That's what he says. And when he talks about loving one another, I guess that means the Romans too, because Jesus says that we should love not only our friends but also our enemies. That is a very hard thing.

Right now, I can see some women pushing up to him with their young children in their arms to ask for a blessing. People do that a lot, but I hope these children are not bothering him, because I really want our group to stay together for as long as possible. It would be so disappointing if Jesus and his friends went on ahead without us.

Not surprisingly, Jesus stops and takes one of the children into his arms. He squats down and pats another child on the head, and he seems to be telling his disciples something about the children. He is smiling and appears to be blessing the children. Although I can't really hear, I can clearly see that Mattathias has gotten himself up close enough to be able to report back to me. He does that, my Mattathias. Unlike most of my friends' husbands, Mattathias talks to me about what he hears and even sometimes asks my opinion. I love him for that! It is unusual for a man to consider a woman a person of value, but now Jesus is talking to the women no differently than he is talking to the men. He is known to do that.

We are walking along a part of the lake now where I can see cliffs on the far side. When I look across the sea, I can see for a great distance. This really is a beautiful land. Everything is a shade of blue and gray and green. Occasional brightly colored flowers wave in the breeze. The road is not too dusty yet since the rains have just recently stopped. And it's nice, this walking and talking with some of the other women from the surrounding villages. At home, we are always working—growing and cooking and preserving our food; gathering water constantly for drinking and for washing our clothes; gathering wood for our fires; tending to any livestock we might have; . . . and tending to the children, of course. There are chances to visit together at the well in the center of town and at the market on days when area farmers bring their produce to town. But this journey is turning out to be a nice change.

Because the lake is narrowing, I can tell that we are coming closer to its southern end where the Sea of Galilee flows into the Jordan River, south past Samaria and into Judea. We don't really associate with the people who live in Samaria, though Jesus is said to have traveled through and even taught in that area. Our rabbi says that the Samaritans haven't been faithful Jews for hundreds of years. They are unrighteous, to be looked down upon, and most people avoid any contact with them. I wonder in fact if we are at greater risk from robbers and bandits on this stretch of our journey. Maybe not, with our numbers growing and everyone staying close together . . . but I still wonder.

Since we have walked for quite some time now, I'm relieved when some women from a nearby village appear up ahead with dried fish, fruit, and some bread to sell. Leave it to food to make Honi come running back to where I am. "I'm starving," is something that I hear him say often, but today I have to agree. I purchase some food for now and some extra for tonight. Although I am sure that we will stop to make our fires and spread our pallets before it gets dark, I'm not sure if we will get another chance to buy supplies before then. I can't see Mattathias in the crowd. He must be mesmerized by Jesus, because he usually comes back to make sure that we have something to eat.

⬦⬦⬦⬦⬦⬦⬦⬦⬦⬦⬦⬦⬦⬦⬦⬦⬦⬦⬦⬦⬦⬦⬦⬦⬦⬦⬦

## 5: Wednesday Evening

The sun is starting to get low in the sky, and I am sure that we will be stopping soon. Suddenly, I hear a great commotion. People are scattering like ants. Then I see them. On the side of the road are some lepers. They are calling out to Jesus to heal them. No one wants to get near them, including me. Where in the world is Honi? I hope he doesn't get too close. I feel sorry for these lepers, and I know that their life of separation is difficult and lonely, but I find myself angry that they are intruding on our walk and risking spreading the disease to someone else. Of course, Jesus walks right up to them and talks to them! I've heard that he doesn't seem to care about touching someone who is unclean.

All of a sudden, the lepers are dancing for joy. They are unwrapping their bandages. Could they have just been healed? Mattathias and I have talked about the possibility of Jesus doing this kind of thing on our journey. We have heard many stories of Jesus' healings. Have I just seen a miracle with my own eyes? The lepers are running back toward their village when one of them stops, turns around, and falls on his knees in front of Jesus. Jesus puts his hand on his head and then the man heads down the path toward Samaria to the south. I hope that Mattathias was close enough to hear what Jesus said. The crowd is obviously impressed. Everyone is talking at once and clapping. I can't wait to hear more about it from my husband.

Up ahead, I can see that our entire group is crossing over the Jordan River. It is shallow here, and because Jews do not often choose to walk through Samaria, we will cross over to the east bank and continue to walk south on that side of the river for most of tomorrow.

After we cross the river, the group finally begins to splinter off into family units to make camp for the night. We are camping right on the bank of the river, so it will be easy enough to go down to get water. There are plenty of trees for shelter in case it rains during the night and plenty of firewood for our fires. Thank goodness Jesus and his friends seem also to be stopping. I can't help laughing to myself, because I can tell that many people want to camp near him . . . but they are trying not to act like it.

"Salome, over here." That's Mattathias calling me and, since Honi has been tired enough to walk with me for the past hour or so, it is easy for us to make our family camp. I take some of the food that I purchased earlier, as well as some lentils and onions that I brought from home, and join the other women at the cookfires. We will have lentil stew, barley bread, and some leftover fish . . . and olives . . . always olives. Luckily, as we eat our dinner and settle down to rest, Mattathias is full of information about the day—what Jesus said, what he did with the lepers. He tells me that Jesus said God's kingdom is about the "first being last and the last being first." He says that Jesus teaches that rich people are no more worthy than poor people and that wealth should be used for God.

"You know Daniel, the merchant?" Mattathias asks me.

I nod. "Yes, he owns more than anyone else we know."

"When Jesus told him he must sell everything that he has in order for his heart to be right, Daniel just sadly walked away. Jesus said it is harder for a rich man to get to the kingdom of heaven than it is for a camel to go through the eye of a needle."

"Wait," I say. "If a rich man is not worthy of God's favor, how can any of us be worthy"?

"That's the point. We all need God. Rich people have a harder time seeing that, I think."

We have had many so-called prophets in our area of Galilee, but none who talked as much about love and humility as Jesus. What Mattathias is telling me is amazing. It confuses me, but it also warms my heart.

"While we were walking, Jesus told a story," Mattathias continues as we settle in for the night. "There was a landowner who went out early in the morning to hire workers for his vineyard, and he agreed to pay them a certain amount. Then he went out around noon and got more workers, and then he went out again close to the end of the day and got even more workers. That evening, when it came time to pay all of the workers, he paid them all the same amount."

"What?" I ask.

"I'm not much more than a day laborer myself," says Mattathias. "When he was telling that story, it made me mad, because I know how unfair that would have seemed if I had been one of the first laborers in the story. But then I thought about how overjoyed

I would have been if I was one of the last laborers. I would feel undeserving . . . but I would be overjoyed."

Smiling, he adds, "I think Jesus was saying that God wants to reward us all equally, that none of us deserves God's blessings any more than anyone else. We shouldn't judge what someone else deserves."

"But that still doesn't seem fair." I can't help it.

"I know." Mattathias shakes his head. "But I think his point is that everything we have in life comes from God anyway."

I am thinking that it is no wonder our religious leaders are starting to fear what Jesus is telling everyone when Mattathias adds, "I have always felt that there is something very, very different about Jesus. You're right when you say that it seems like he looks into your soul when he talks to you. And his patience with the people is amazing, not to mention the fact that he knows more Scripture than anyone I've ever heard of. He always has the answer to everything. It's strange to think that he was just a carpenter."

We muse for a while about the revolutionary ideas that Jesus teaches. Honi is already asleep. Even though my mind is full, my body is tired, so like everyone else I fall asleep under the stars.

<><><><><><><><><><><><><><><><><><><><><><><><>

## 6:Thursday Morning

I see dew on the grass, but I can tell that the day will be warm. The days have been growing longer and warmer for a few weeks now. The river is gentle here, and several people are down in the water refreshing themselves for the day. Some of the women are collecting the water that we'll carry in pouches made of animal skins, and they are packing up the leftover food for the small meal that we will have later this morning as we walk. I see that Honi is over by the area where the cooking fires were the night before. He is playing with some boys who are also walking with their families. It's nice that families are sharing their supplies. Most people are happy and helpful so far. Maybe Jesus' message is rubbing off on us. We should pass through Jericho today and then hopefully make it to Mariam and Yohanan's house by sundown the following day before the Sabbath begins. I'm sure we will. Everyone on this walk has the same deadline.

Sooner than I expect, people start packing up and preparing to leave. "Hurry up, Salome," Mattathias says. Honi never stays right with me anyway, so I hurry with Mattathias to get as close to Jesus as possible today, and before we know it, we are walking in a group of men and women who are talking and laughing with Jesus. He is an ordinary man in appearance. His hands are strong and calloused. His hair and beard are dark like my husband's, for he is still a young man. He is about the same height as Mattathias, and other than his amazing eyes, there is nothing obviously special about him. It's strange that he's not married, though, which is very unusual for a man his age. I guess he probably couldn't support a wife with all of the traveling around that he does these days. I steal a look at him and flush when he smiles at me. What unnerving depth there is in his eyes. He almost makes you feel like you are part of his family.

We walk for several hours, and the mood is light until Jesus says, "We are going up to Jerusalem, and the Son of Man will be delivered over to the chief priests and the teachers of the law. They will condemn him to death and hand him over to the Gentiles, who will mock him, spit on him, flog him, and kill him. Three days later, he will rise."

Of course, the people walking near Jesus erupt in protest. No one seems to understand what he means when he says that what has been written by the prophets must be fulfilled.

Is he talking about himself, I wonder? Some people may be irritated by him, but would they actually condemn him to death? And how does he know that? Why would he continue on this journey if that were true? And then something amazing happens. Jesus turns his head, looks right into my eyes, and gives a slight nod. He looks sad but determined.

I gasp. "Mattathias, he knows what I'm thinking again! He looked straight at me like he could hear my thoughts. Did you see that?"

I stop in my tracks, but Mattathias has continued to walk, and more and more people are pushing between us. I have to hurry to catch up. Is there going to be trouble? Surely, he can't mean that he expects to be killed! And what was that about rising from the dead? Only God himself can conquer death!

"What did he just say?" a woman asks me. I don't know her. She must have joined our group along the way. She is holding a small child who is secured to her body with her shawl. Like all of us women, she has her head covered, but I can tell that she is young and pretty.

"I think that he was saying that he is going to be arrested in Jerusalem and that he will be killed but will rise again in three days." I shake my head and shrug my shoulders, because who could begin to understand what he means by that.

"I hope he is not arrested," the woman says. "I know that he says challenging things, but I wouldn't worry too much about him. God's power is definitely on him."

"I've felt twice now that he could tell what I was thinking," I replied. "But I can't quite understand who he is and where his knowledge comes from."

"All I know is that I was visiting my mother last year when Jesus came to her village to teach," she said. "It was hot, and since her neighbor has a large house, we crowded into their front room to hear Jesus speak. There were even several Pharisees and teachers there. He was saying something about bearing good fruit when we heard some men up on the roof. Jesus stopped talking, and we all watched as the men removed the thick, woven mats from the roof and lowered their friend down, so that he was lying right in front of Jesus. Jesus looked at the crippled man and said, 'Friend, your sins are forgiven.' Of course, the Pharisees did not like that and immediately started whispering among themselves."

"What happened?" I asked her.

"Jesus asked them which was easier, to forgive sins or to tell the man to stand up and walk. He claimed that he *did* have authority on earth to forgive sins, and then he told the man to stand up, take his mat, and go home. So he did! I saw it myself," she exclaims.

I am shaking my head in wonder and confusion. Jesus keeps calling himself the "Son of Man," which is an obvious reference to Daniel in the Scriptures. If he can forgive sins, can he conquer death? Is he ushering in God's kingdom now? What does it all mean?

## 7:Thursday Afternoon

Since we left Capernaum, there have been animals walking with us. There are quite a few people who are bringing small animals with them for sacrifice, and I can see that Honi and his friends are darting in and out of a small flock of sheep, to the irritation of their owner. I have been keeping one eye on Honi. He is filthy, of course. I will be embarrassed when we get to Mariam's. Her husband Yohanan is a tailor, and they are wealthier than we are. For some reason, that has always made me feel a little self-conscious. I remember that their house has several rooms, one of which is Yohanan's workroom, and they have two floors as well as the usual flat, open rooftop. They have a table where they eat their meals and several chairs and benches. They have a large open-air courtyard in the back that belongs only to them, and Mariam even has a clay oven out by her fire pit. There is a large, enclosed room upstairs that Yohanan uses for storage, but they also rent that room out during the many festivals that occur in Jerusalem. Their house is made of stone instead of mud bricks, and Mariam has several carved chests where she keeps supplies and extra clothing. She will be warm and welcoming, though. We were very close as children and have seen each other as often as possible through the years.

At home, I have several close friends, but most of them have many children. I have only Honi. We wanted more children, of course, but that was not to be. I have learned to find joy in the voices of my nieces and nephews as they play in the courtyard, and I am grateful every single day that if I could have only one child, that child is the perfect boy that is my Honi! Mariam also has only John Mark. We have many things in common, and I am looking forward to seeing her again.

The men who are closest to Jesus, and whom he has called his special disciples, are an interesting group. Several of them are, of course, fishermen, and some of them I believe are craftsmen. At least one of them is reported to be a zealot, a violent man who has been fighting against the Romans for years. Mattathias tells me that one of them is actually a tax collector who works for the Roman governor. Somehow, Jesus has been able to inspire them all to work together and, by all appearances, to care for one another. Peter is married. I've met his wife. I don't know if the others are married or not. A few of them can evidently read and write. They are a strange combination of simple men, mostly from Galilee, who spend their time traveling with Jesus and learning from what he is teaching. They help to control the crowd when it gets too large, and they openly talk about the miracles that they have seen performed. But they do not look like an imposing group of powerful men who are going to help Jesus lead any type of revolution. They can't even seem to agree among themselves about exactly who Jesus is.

From what I hear, our priests and elders are irritated by the way that Jesus takes control of the conversation and seems to know more than they do. His message that it is the humble and the servant who will be rewarded, not the outwardly pious, threatens their position of authority. But I don't see how Jesus and his disciples are doing any harm.

Anyway, what an amazing day it has been. I have been able to observe Jesus and his friends most of the day as we've walked along. My feet are sore and my throat is parched, but I am so thankful for such a full day. I wonder what tomorrow will hold.

Obviously, we will have to stop for one more night soon, but finding a good place to camp might be a challenge. It definitely won't be as comfortable as the place we were blessed with last night. We have crossed back over to the west side of the Jordan River now that we are past Samaritan land, and the area is growing rockier and drier as we head away from the water.

Jesus is talking about the fact that no one will know the time when God will return but that we must always be prepared. He says when that time comes, it will be clear to everyone on earth. I wonder what he means. He says that "loving God and loving other people" is the most important thing in this life—more important than religious rules or rituals. He tells everyone that, if we know him, we will know God and will have even seen God. There is something so powerful in his words. I can feel it.

I'm surprised when two of Jesus' disciples get into an argument. I know Peter because he and my brothers have become friends. Peter used to live in the neighboring village of Bethsaida. Since my brothers are also fishermen, they have gotten to know one another well. I also know a couple of the other disciples, Zebedee's sons; they too are fishermen. Those two brothers are the ones who have been arguing. With a deep sigh, Jesus stops and tells them, "All who exalt themselves will be humbled, and all who humble themselves will be exalted."

They were arguing over who would get to sit at Jesus' right and left hands in heaven. He has basically just told them that the most lowly among them, the ones who are willing to serve others, will be the ones exalted in heaven. "That's what he was saying yesterday," Mattathias whispers as the group starts to walk on, clearly chastened. "It's almost the opposite of what the elders teach."

Time to stop for the night.

〰〰〰〰〰〰〰〰〰〰〰〰〰〰〰〰〰〰

# 8: Friday Morning

As we approach Jericho, we start to see more Roman soldiers. I know that's because we are getting closer to Jerusalem. A herd of goats is grazing on the opposite side of the road under the semi-watchful eyes of some young boys. The contrast between the soldiers' threatening presence and this peaceful scene is striking. Our land has been occupied by foreign powers for generation upon generation. No wonder people are ready for our Messiah to come to set us free so that we can enjoy the blessings that God has promised.

"Jesus, son of David, have mercy on me," someone shouts. I see a blind beggar by the side of the road. Some of Jesus' followers try to quiet the man, because they don't want him to slow down their journey. But sure enough, Jesus stops and tells his disciples to call the man over. The man jumps up and with some help makes his way over to Jesus. When Jesus asks the man what he wants Jesus to do for him, the beggar says, "Lord, I want to see." So Jesus reaches out to him and says something about his faith having healed him. The next thing I know, the man is waving his arms with excitement. He can obviously see now, and everyone around here must know him, because as we walk into the city, people are calling out, "Bartimaeus can see."

"Bartimaeus has been healed by Jesus of Nazareth."

Mattathias just looks at me in disbelief. "Am I crazy that this is starting to seem normal?"

Jericho is lovelier than I remembered. Despite the desert and the rock surrounding it, the town is very green and trees line the road. As word of Bartimaeus spreads, more and more people are starting to climb up into those trees to try and get a glimpse of Jesus. I know how they feel. With the crowd growing, we are falling further behind, and it's harder to hear what is happening. I can see that at one tree, Jesus stops, looks up, and calls someone down. He puts his arm around the man, and along with a few of his disciples, they head off into town.

"He went home with Zacchaeus, the tax collector," someone says indignantly.

People start to scatter. Since we are hungry and tired, most of us sit down to eat some dried fruit and goat cheese that we have brought with us. Although some people are hurrying on to try to get to Jerusalem before sundown, it is obvious that many of us are waiting around to see if Jesus will come back to finish walking with us. Most of his close disciples are still here, and they look as confused as everyone else. We relax for a few minutes. Luckily, after we eat and rest a little, we see Jesus returning. Zacchaeus appears to be happy. Jesus just smiles when the tax collector starts giving coins to people in the crowd. That's the first time I've ever seen a tax collector give money back to people!

When things calm down, and without anyone coordinating it, our group resumes walking together toward Jerusalem. We will have to hurry to get to my cousin's house before sundown.

◇◇◇◇◇◇◇◇◇◇◇◇◇◇◇◇◇◇◇◇◇◇◇◇◇◇◇◇◇◇◇◇◇◇◇◇◇◇◇◇

# 9:Friday Afternoon

We have been walking uphill for some time now. Gone are the lush banks of the Jordan. Now we are surrounded by rock and dust. The path has grown narrower, and our group must spread farther apart. Luckily, Mattathias and I can still hear Jesus even if I can't always see past the people in front of us.

I have learned on this journey that Jesus tells many stories, some with obvious lessons, some a little more confusing. Now he starts a story about a nobleman who owned many servants but wanted to go on a trip to another land. The nobleman called three of his servants and gave them each three month's wages. "Put this money to work," he said, "until I come back." After a time, when he did come back, the first servant said that he had put the money to work and had doubled his master's money. The second servant said that he had also put his master's money to work and had earned a profit. But the third servant didn't respect the nobleman and hadn't bothered to invest what the master had entrusted to him. He hadn't tried to do anything good with it. It seems that the third servant had just gone about his own business while the master was gone and had forgotten what he was supposed to do.

The master commended the first two servants and rewarded them, but he rebuked the third servant. The first two servants were given even more responsibility and more privileges. They grew closer to the nobleman and were honored in his household. But the third servant was thrown out and had no part of the master's kingdom.

For the next several hours, we walk and talk about that nobleman, about how happy those first two servants must have been that they were good trustees of what their master had entrusted to them, and about how regretful the third servant must have been that he had wasted his opportunity.

I've been noticing for the past few miles that several people who have joined our group are carrying small animals that they plan to sacrifice at the temple, mostly birds in woven cages. Mattathias will buy a dove for us at the temple this week for our sacrifice, because we didn't have anything that we could bring with us on our journey. As Jews have done since before the time of Moses, we will offer a perfect, unblemished sacrificial animal. This is our way of asking God to place upon the animal all of the punishment that we deserve for the things we have done to separate ourselves from God. We will pray that God accepts that sacrifice in our place and that our relationship with him will be restored.

The sun is getting low in the sky when we finally see Jerusalem up ahead. The city wall is so much larger than I had remembered, and the temple is magnificent. It towers over the rest of the city and gleams white in the fading sunlight. Bethany and Bethphage sit just a little further on, and it is with regret that we see Jesus and his closest friends turn off of the path and away from the rest of us. When we were eating at noon in Jericho, I overheard some of Jesus' disciples discussing the fact that they were going to stay with some friends in Bethany for the week. It sounded like they will stay in Bethany each night and walk into Jerusalem each day, however, so maybe we will see Jesus again in the city. For now, we hurry down the mountainside, across the valley, and through the imposing city gates.

Jerusalem is so crowded, and the streets are so narrow. They wind around the stone buildings in the most confusing manner.

Honi is having the time of his life. There are Roman soldiers everywhere we look, and there seem to be people here from so many different places. We can hear people calling out in strange languages and see people dressed in strange clothing. Small shops line the streets, and people keep grabbing my arms as weavers, dyers, and potters reach out to try and convince us that we need to buy what they are offering. But it is almost sundown, and even though there is so much to see, I can't wait to get to Mariam's house to tell her about all of the amazing things that Jesus has said and done on this journey. Mattathias seems just as eager. He has always liked Yohanan and enjoys having another man that he can talk with comfortably.

When we get there, Honi and John Mark are awkward at first, but they soon are laughing and talking like twelve-year-old boys do. Honi has always been able to make friends easily. He is full of confidence, but still able to be kind, and I am proud of him.

We are of course all very hungry. Mariam has prepared a wonderful Sabbath meal for us. I rush to help her lay everything out and prepare the table for the evening. Tomorrow will be a restful day when we can share our stories with one another and catch up with all that has happened. We will stay home, there will be no work to be done, and we will reflect on our blessings. I feel happy as well as excited . . . and there is an anticipation in my heart that I can't explain.

## 10:Sunday Morning

On the first day of the week, Mattathias and Yohanan decide to take the boys to the temple because, even though the boys are too young to enter the men's court, our men still have so much that they want to show their sons. I would like to see the temple also, but Mariam really wants me to go with her to see her garden. She assures me that we'll have plenty of opportunities to visit the area in the temple where women are allowed to worship.

"We will see you later today," the men say as they round up the boys and head out the door. Mariam and I pick up our baskets and walk in the opposite direction toward the city wall. I have been envious of Mariam's large house, but I am not envious of the fact that she must walk to where her garden is outside of the city. At home, I have my small garden right beside our house, and our mule is kept right there with us. Yohanan and Mariam may have the excitement of the city, but their lives do have their own complications.

We gather what we need from the plot of land that Mariam is cultivating and visit with the other women who are doing the same. The communal garden itself takes up quite a bit of land on a large flat area outside of the city gates. It seems that different families from inside the city can designate a plot of land which will be theirs to tend. Mariam grows many of the things that my mother-in-law and I grow at home. Because Jerusalem sits up higher from the sea than our part of Galilee, it is cooler and drier than I am used to. It's nice.

Mariam introduces me to a friend of hers, Leah, and the conversation keeps coming back to Jesus. Leah says that her husband went out to Bethany early this morning, because he knows a man named Lazarus and wants to see the man who raised him from the dead not so long ago. I hadn't heard this story, so Leah tells me how one of Jesus' close friends, Lazarus from Bethany, had died.

Then, after several days, Jesus brought him back to life. In front of many witnesses! Leah's husband took several of his friends and went out to Bethany "to investigate." She smiles and shrugs her shoulders. It seems that everyone is curious about Jesus.

When we turn to head home, we hear shouting and clapping echoing across the valley. A large crowd of people are starting to line the road that leads from Bethany up into the city. "What do you think is happening?" I ask Mariam.

She shrugs her shoulders. "I don't know. They seem to be celebrating. They seem happy."

We stand there in the sun. As the crowd grows nearer, we can hear them shouting, "Hosanna. Blessed is he who comes in the name of the Lord." We see people running from the city out to meet them and joining in the cries of "Blessed is the coming kingdom of our father David" and "Hosanna in the highest."

People are waving palm branches and laying their garments down on the road. Then we see Jesus. He is riding on a donkey surrounded by his disciples and the crowds of people. "Salome, there's a small rise beside the road up closer to the city wall. Let's get closer if we can," Mariam says, as she pulls me through the throng and up to a good spot where we can watch what is happening. Below us, two men are talking excitedly.

"I heard that he had his disciples go and find a colt for him to ride into the city and that it happened exactly like the prophet Zechariah said it would."

"What do you mean?"

"You know . . . the prophecy that our king will come riding on a donkey, lowly but victorious. This man, Jesus from Nazareth

. . . everyone thinks he's the one, the one who will kick out the Romans and bring the glory of our kingdom back."

Mariam and I look at one another. We are excited, but we are also confused. We all talked late into the night last night about what people have heard, and about what Mattathias and I had seen on our walk, but it didn't sound like Jesus was planning an armed revolt to us.

"It seems like he talks more about love and peace and justice than he does about anything else. People say that he often calls himself our 'shepherd,'" Mariam says.

I agree. "And his eyes. I wish you could see his eyes, Mariam. When he looks at you, the impression you get is that he knows you and loves you and will somehow make everything all right."

"But look at him now," my cousin replies, and when I do, I see him pass through the city gates with his head held high but with a fearsome, determined sadness on his face.

It takes a while for the crowds to disperse, but when we can, we walk back to Mariam's house and spend all afternoon talking about what we have seen. Mariam is fortunate enough to have two servants, a young man who helps Yohanan in his garment business, and his wife, Sarah, who helps Mariam in the house. I am grateful to Sarah. She has already washed our clothing from our journey. For a while, the three of us work together to prepare the evening meal. Sarah is shy about speaking, but she does say that she has also heard of Jesus from Nazareth and that she knows that he teaches compassion. He says that the kingdom of God is for everyone. "Even servants," she says with a smile.

"Yohanan heard him tell a story once," Mariam tells us. "It was about a wise man who built his house on a rock and a foolish man who built his house on sand. The wise man built his life on God's purposes but the foolish man built his life on temporary things."

"I have heard about that story," adds Sarah. "When the storms of life came, the wise man had God's strength to sustain him, but the foolish man did not have anything that lasted."

It occurs to me that Sarah, despite being a lowly servant, is wise and kind. She is exactly the kind of person that Jesus has been talking about the past couple of days.

<hr>

## 11:Sunday Afternoon

"You will not believe what happened," the men call out when they get back. Honi and John Mark can't wait to tell the story. "Jesus turned over the money changers' tables and money went flying everywhere. He turned over some other tables too where people were selling animals for sacrifice. We could hear the noise, and people were scattering to get out of the way."

"He got very angry at the merchants who were treating the temple only as a place of business," Mattathias explained.

The boys couldn't hide their glee at anything that the religious leaders wouldn't like. "I thought you said he was a peaceful man who teaches about love," John Mark snickers.

Shaking his head, Mattathias says, "Son, I was surprised too. But those merchants have been taking advantage of people for far too long, charging unreasonable prices for sacrificial animals and creating unfair rules about what is acceptable and what is not. Everyone knows that they are corrupt, but our religious leaders have been looking the other way for years."

Yohanan tells the boys to sit down and then says, "Jesus used the words of the prophet Jeremiah today when he said, 'My house will be called a house of prayer, but you are making it a den of robbers.' When Jeremiah used those words hundreds of years ago, he was telling the people that God didn't care about their empty shows of piety and careless sacrifices. Instead, he wanted his people to take care of the immigrant and the orphan and the widow. He was telling the people that God was fed up with their disobedience and their shallow faith and that there would be consequences. And there were. Shortly after that, the temple was destroyed and our people were carried away into Babylonian exile."

"Yes, it was a pretty clear message today," adds Mattathias. "Jesus was telling the temple leaders, the merchants—and even the ordinary people—that none of us can ignore God's command to care for the weak and then claim that our prayers and our sacrifices and our rituals will make everything all right with God. Do you understand?"

## 12:Sunday Evening

The boys are in bed. The four of us talk about the events of the day. We have heard Jesus preach about the meek inheriting the earth and the comfort that is coming for those who mourn. He is not hesitant to call out the powerful on their hypocrisy. But will he use his power against Rome? No one is quite sure what to make of him.

"And what about quoting the prophet Jeremiah?" I ask. "Is he threatening that the temple will once again be destroyed?"

Yohanan shakes his head. "I don't know. But he sure made the priests angry today."

Chuckling, Mattathias adds, "They were already angry when they saw that great procession coming up the hill and the crowd claiming that Jesus is the long-awaited Messiah. They can't conceive of God working through someone other than them."

Mattathias and Yohanan talk for a while about what Jesus taught today in the temple and about how upset the priests were that he continued to let his followers treat him like a king. They had heard some of the Pharisees arguing about who Jesus really was and what they should do about him.

"I feel the truth of what he says, Yohanan. But I can't understand what he is planning to do with all of these followers. Word is spreading far and wide about what he preaches and about the miracles he performs. But what comes next?" Mattathias wonders.

As Yohanan blows out the candles, he tells us what we already know. "The whole city is worked up because they think that Jesus' revolt against Rome may come at any minute."

<hr>

## 13:Monday

The next morning, Sarah agrees to keep an eye on the boys, and Mariam and I walk with Yohanan and Mattathias up to the temple. We want to see for ourselves. The temple is grand, even the outer Gentile court and the middle women's court, and we enjoy the sights and the atmosphere. What an amazing place! It is easy to tell when Jesus and his followers appear, because the people move to try and catch a glimpse of him as if he were royalty. Sometimes it's hard to catch what he is saying, but most people are quiet enough and are trying themselves to listen. Every once in a while, someone asks a question, and Jesus as usual tells a story in reply. Right now, he is talking about a man who had two sons. He asked them both to go to work in the vineyard for him. One said that he would. He said all the right things and behaved politely, but he got caught up in his own pursuits and didn't ever go to work for his father. The other one was rude and said that he didn't want to go work, but then he repented and went to the vineyard like his father had asked.

When Jesus asks, "Which son actually did his father's will?" everyone knows it was the son who, despite his complaining, went to work as his father had asked. It is truly fascinating to watch Jesus with the people. He looks at each one as if they are the most important person in the world. I know that look. He is a very learned rabbi, of course, but with his words he can spark an understanding in me that is new and wonderful. He reveals the Scriptures to have a deeper meaning than I ever imagined. What a commanding presence he has. No wonder people listen to him!

"The kingdom of heaven is like a king who prepared a wedding banquet for his son," Jesus is saying. He tells the story of a wedding banquet where the people who were invited didn't want to come. They couldn't be bothered to respond to the king's invitation. So the king invited other people off of the street—plain, ordinary people, acceptable and unacceptable alike. He even provided them with the appropriate wedding clothes to wear, so that they could enjoy the banquet with due respect. It seems that all those who responded with appreciation and effort were welcomed into the banquet, but those who didn't bother to make the effort were thrown out.

The crowd is growing, and it includes men and women, which is an unusual but welcome sight. It is obvious that the priests and the teachers of the law are irritated by both the crowd's size and its makeup. They didn't like that last story that he told, either! I can see that some of the disciples are urging Jesus to avoid insulting these leaders, but instead he jumps up on a table and begins yet another story.

"I could listen to him all day," someone standing next to us says. I notice that the priest that overhears this comment is scowling. "Look at the elders," Yohanan says to Mattathias with a nudge. "They don't like the implications of these teachings." Sure enough, some of the Pharisees push forward to have a conversation with Jesus that we can't hear. But then, he lifts his voice and says to them sternly, "Truly I tell you, the tax collectors and prostitutes are entering the kingdom of God ahead of you." It's becoming more and more evident that what Jesus is teaching about God's kingdom is very different from what our elders teach. He is angering them, and I am starting to worry.

Hours have gone by without us even realizing it. Jesus is mesmerizing. But we are hungry and tired and need to check on the boys, so Mattathias and Yohanan go to meet a friend of Yohanan's, and Mariam and I head home. Since we walk along in silence, I assume that Mariam is also thinking about what Jesus said today. We have always been taught to be in awe of the elders with their wisdom, fine robes, and authority. If God isn't pleased with them, what does that mean?

"How about the story of the wicked tenants?" Mariam murmurs. And somehow, I feel like I understand.

"I think that's meant to teach that all we have been entrusted with is God's. God has given us everything that we have. We can't forget that and start thinking that it is ours to do with as we please."

She stares into the distance for a while and then nods. "I'm glad you are here, Salome." We push through her door and into the house.

◇◇◇◇◇◇◇◇◇◇◇◇◇◇◇◇◇◇◇◇◇◇◇◇◇◇◇◇◇

## 14:Wednesday

The past two days have been busy with baking special bread and preparing food that Mariam can send to be sold in the marketplace. Many, many people are in the city for the Passover celebration, and food vendors are everywhere. Mariam says that she usually makes a good deal of extra money each year during this time. A friend of hers has a stall on one of the busiest streets. Also, even though no one has yet rented their upstairs room, Mariam wants to be prepared in case a family does want to use it over Passover. So in spite of the fact that all I want to do is go back to the temple grounds to listen to Jesus again, I stay and help her. The boys are full of stories about King Herod's imposing palace and the soldiers who are everywhere in Jerusalem. John Mark has introduced Honi to some of his friends, and they spend a great deal of time playing outside the city walls.

Each evening, Yohanan and Mattathias come home with stories about Jesus. "Today the Pharisees and even the Sadducees questioned Jesus' authority and tried to trick him with questions about John the Baptist and about marriage after the resurrection."

I laugh. "The Sadducees don't even believe in a resurrection."

"Exactly," Yohanan says with a grin. "They are just trying to find something to trap him with."

Mattathias chimes in. "They asked him whether or not it is right to pay Roman taxes to Caesar, and he turned it around on them."

I think our husbands would pick up and follow Jesus with very little encouragement themselves. They are always debating his teachings and speculating about what might be to come.

## 15: Wednesday Evening

It seems like all we do when the boys go to bed is sit around and talk about Jesus and what he is teaching. It's all anyone in the city seems to be doing this week. The men tell us a story about Jesus supposedly cursing a fig tree and then using it to talk about the power of faith. Then they tell us about a teacher of the law who came up and asked Jesus what the greatest commandment is.

"What did he say?" I ask.

"He said that the greatest commandment is to love God with all of your being and to love your neighbor as you love yourself."

We all nod. That sounds consistent with what we've heard from him all along.

"Today, he actually called the religious leaders 'empty vessels,' all show and no substance. A poor widow woman had been in the outer court praying, and as we walked by, she went over and put a tiny offering in the temple treasury. Jesus stopped, pointed her out, and said that her offering was more pleasing to God than all of their showy offerings put together."

"The people are getting restless too," Yohanan points out. "They were expecting something more revolutionary to happen after that grand entrance the other day. I think they are disappointed that Jesus seems to be doing nothing but teaching. We heard a lot more grumbling today about 'who does he think he is ?' and 'when is he going to do something?'"

"I saw one of his disciples talking with the chief priests, and even he looked frustrated." Mattathias lets out a deep sigh and shakes his head. "I love what Jesus teaches, but he's said several times that he must be handed over and crucified, and I'm afraid that might be the way things are going, based on the growing sentiment out there."

We are sitting at the table talking about the growing danger Jesus is putting himself in when there is a knock on the door. It is Yohanan's neighbor, and he has even more stories to share. He says that Jesus had dinner at Simon the Leper's house out in Bethany last night and that one of the women in his group poured an expensive bottle of perfume on him. Jesus, instead of rebuking her, commended her and said she had done the right thing. Shrugging his shoulders, he says, "I heard that it was almost as if she was anointing him king."

"But," he adds, "then I saw him and his disciples leaving the temple this afternoon. When one of the disciples said something about how beautiful the temple is, Jesus said: 'Every stone will be thrown down.' I heard it myself."

Yohanan's neighbor is upset, because he can't decide whether Jesus has come to rescue the Jewish people or just to make more trouble. Why is he talking about the temple being destroyed?

Mariam and I leave the men to their discussion, and it seems very late when Mattathias lies down on our pallet and says, "We didn't want to say this in front of Yohanan's neighbor, but we met some of Jesus' disciples today, and they mentioned that they may need a place to celebrate their meal tomorrow night. Yohanan told them that he has that large room upstairs, and he could host them if they need it."

"How exciting." I sit up but he pulls me back down beside him.

"We'll see. I'm not sure we want to be in the middle of whatever is happening." Mattathias seems pensive, but I hope Jesus and his followers will come and use our extra room.

<hr>

## 16:Thursday Morning

Sarah's husband comes in with the large clay pot of water that we need for the day. He is followed by two of Jesus' disciples.

"These men say that their master needs to use the upstairs room for tonight's meal."

Yohanan nods and jumps up to greet the disciples whom he met yesterday. He and Mattathias take the men up the outside staircase and show them the room upstairs that Mariam, Sarah, and I cleaned out this week. I assume that they discuss the price, and when they come back down, it is all agreed. Although we women now have quite a bit of extra food to prepare, none of us can contain our excitement at the fact that Jesus himself will be in our house tonight.

## 17: Thursday Evening

Finally, the day is drawing to a close, the house is clean, and both our Passover meal and the meal for upstairs have been prepared. Sarah has agreed to serve in the upper room, and I'm almost jealous, because I would love to be able to hear what is said there tonight. We can hear talk and laughter as they approach. Jesus and twelve of his closest disciples are arriving.

"It is an honor to have you here, teacher," Yohanan says as he directs them up the outside staircase. In the upstairs room sits a low table with couches for the men to rest on. We have put down a clean rug and set out water bowls and towels, so they can clean their hands, as well as candles and incense to light and freshen the room. All of the men are courteous. Peter, who recognizes Mattathias and me, stops briefly to say hello. For the rest of the evening, Sarah is kept busy running up and down the stairs, but her face is glowing, and I can't wait to ask her what is being said. We try to concentrate on our meal, because the boys are almost of age and must learn how to carry on our traditions as the men of faith that we know they will become. At some point, we hear one of the disciples run down the stairs and away, but the rest of them remain for quite some time. When they leave, they are somber. They are not laughing and joking as they were upon their arrival. Jesus thanks Mariam, Peter nods to Mattathias, and then they are gone.

"Sarah, what happened up there? What did they talk about?" Yohanan asks. Sarah speaks so quietly that it is hard to hear her, but with encouragement from Mariam, she starts to tell us about their conversation.

"Jesus said that he was going to have to go away and that the disciples couldn't come with him yet, but that they would see him again soon. He said that they would suffer for him but that he would send a holy spirit that will help them to understand everything. He promised them that this holy spirit will strengthen them when they need it." She shrugs and says, "And then he washed each of the disciples' feet. When they protested, he said that they must serve one another in a like manner."

Looking at Mattathias and me, she adds, "Jesus told your friend Peter that he will deny him three times before the rooster crows tomorrow morning. Oh, and when he broke the bread for them to share and passed the cup, he said something about it being his body and his blood. He told them that he was making a new covenant and that they should remember him when they eat and drink."

"We heard someone leave early?" I question.

"Yes, but I don't know why. Jesus said something to one of them and he just left abruptly."

She shares some more about the personalities of the disciples and a discussion among them about which one of them is greatest, but we can tell that she is tired, and Mariam says Sarah has never been comfortable talking too much, so we let her go.

## 18:Thursday Night

Honi is in the corner of the main room, sound asleep on the floor. We had put the boys to hard work today, getting furniture moved and everything ready for Jesus and his group. It looks like he is worn out. It is definitely time for bed, and Mattathias and I decide to let Honi sleep where he is. Not until sometime later do I hear Yohanan in the next room waking up Honi and asking him if he knows where John Mark is. When Honi comes into our room after that, he is worried that John Mark will get into trouble. "I don't know where he went," Honi promises. "But he did tell me that he sometimes sneaks out at night to wander around." I can't help wondering, as I fall back asleep, if Honi would also be out there wandering if he hadn't been so tired tonight.

It is sometime past midnight. I hear a commotion and realize that John Mark has come home and is upset. He has woken up his parents and is talking loudly.

"They arrested him! A bunch of soldiers came out of the city gate, across the valley and into that garden they call Gethsemane, where Jesus and his disciples had been praying. It looked like someone came up to Jesus and kissed his hand. Then one of Jesus' disciples took a sword and cut off someone's ear. And then things went crazy! The soldiers were all starting to draw their swords when Jesus stepped forward and said to let the disciples go."

He is shaking, and I can tell that Mariam is both angry and relieved that he is ok. At this point, all of us including Honi are in the main room. Yohanan brings John Mark some goat's milk and asks him to start over and tell us everything that happened. Evidently, John Mark had slipped out and followed Jesus and his disciples over to the Garden of Gethsemane.

"I can't believe you went so far in the middle of the night!" Mariam cries. "This is not the end of that discussion. But go on."

John Mark says that Jesus and his disciples were there for quite some time. Jesus went a few yards away to pray, and the disciples were spread out waiting for him. A few of them were sleeping. He said that it looked like Jesus was in agony for a while, and then finally he seemed to be at peace. When the soldiers came out of the city gates, they were carrying torches and not even trying to be secretive.

"Jesus and his disciples just watched them come," he said. "It looked like some of his friends were trying to get him to disappear over the Mount of Olives and into the desert, but Jesus just stood there and watched them come. He said something about the prophecy from Isaiah being fulfilled."

John Mark was crying now, which I know embarrassed him, but he was obviously afraid. "I just kept hiding," he cried, "until the soldiers left with him. I don't know where the disciples went. I just ran home as fast as I could. I am so, so sorry."

We are all drained and sad. Mariam and Yohanan take John Mark into their room, and Mattathias takes Honi into ours. I just sit there because I am devastated that Jesus has been arrested. I clearly remember what he said that day on the road. He said that he would be turned over to the authorities and crucified, but then he would rise from the dead on the third day. Is that possible? How did he know what would happen, and why does he think he can conquer death? I fear that all of this is going wrong, and I cry because I can't help caring for him. Even though we haven't spoken much since that day when I was weeping in my garden, I have felt somehow that he cares deeply about me and my family. Mattathias has felt it too.

Of course, I sleep poorly. I'm sure we all do.

<hr />

# 19:Friday Early Morning

Right before dawn there is a pounding at the door. I am already awake, and I rush to see who it is. It is Peter. He is distraught, and I can hardly understand what he is saying. Everyone is awake now, and Yohanan demands to know what is happening.

"He was right," Peter sobs. "He said that I would deny knowing him three times before the rooster crowed and, even knowing that, I still did it. I was so afraid that they would arrest me too. How can my faith be so weak? I am so ashamed."

For the second time that night, Yohanan prepares a calming drink—this time not milk—and we gather around to hear what Peter has to say.

"We know that Jesus has been arrested." Mattathias brings Peter a bench and gently pushes him down.

"John got us into the courtyard at Annas' and Caiaphas' compound," Peter says shakily, "and I sat down by a fire where several of the high priest's servants were warming themselves. When the first person asked me if I knew Jesus, I didn't even think about what I was saying. We could hear Jesus being questioned. All of the elders, the chief priests, and even many of the teachers of the law had gathered there . . . to find something to charge him with, I'm sure."

Peter is breathing heavily. "They even had several 'witnesses' step forward to make claims that they could use, but those people couldn't get their stories straight, and I could see that the leaders were getting frustrated. I heard them ask him if he was the Messiah, the Son of God, and he used the very words that God used with Moses, 'I AM.' He even quoted Daniel and claimed to be the one 'sitting at the right hand of power and coming on the clouds of heaven.'"

Yohanan gasps. "He is claiming to be God himself!"

We all shake our heads in wonder.

"There have been moments when I thought so," Peter sighs. "But how can the Son of God have been arrested? They were even mocking him and spitting on him. I know that they were about to take him to Pilate, because they were all claiming 'blasphemy.' They want Pilate to crucify him. By then, I had denied even knowing him a second time." Peter bows his head.

"Then someone recognized me as the one who cut off Malchus' ear, and as soon as the denial was out of my mouth, the rooster crowed again. Jesus looked straight at me as they were leading him off, but he smiled at me with understanding and sympathy . . . sympathy, of all things . . . in his eyes. He still loves me. Oh, Jesus, I am so, so sorry."

Peter, despondent, just sits there with his head in his hands, and I'm not sure how much time passes with each of us lost in our thoughts. Even the boys are somber and still.

## 20:Friday, Midday

Peter has left to try and meet up with John to find out what is happening with Jesus. About thirty minutes earlier, Yohanan's and Mariam's neighbor, the man we met the other night, had stuck his head in and said that there was a large crowd gathering outside of Herod's palace.

"Please, can we just go see?" Honi and John Mark beg.

"We have to, Yohanan," Mariam adds. "We can't just ignore the situation."

So on a beautiful, sunny day, we join the many other people who are also walking to the plaza in front of the palace. Even from a distance, we can hear the crowd. When we get to the square, we are amazed at the number of people gathered there. They are not shouting and calling for Jesus' release like I expected. They are murmuring and debating one another.

"I don't know who he really is, but he is obviously not kicking out the Romans any time soon. I think he's a fraud."

"But he fulfilled the prophecy by riding into the city on a donkey a few days ago, and he speaks with such wisdom. I still think something will happen."

"I heard that his own disciple betrayed him. Look at him, he's helpless."

I stretch up on my tiptoes and can see Jesus. He is bound but dressed in royal robes, and it looks like he has a circle of thorns around his head like a crown. He has obviously been beaten. "Mattathias," pulling him close so that he can hear me, "is that blood running down the side of his face?"

"It looks like it. He is in bad shape. This isn't good."

The religious leaders and the high priest are standing off to the side on the platform where Jesus stands, and they start calling out, "Blasphemy. Crucify him." It begins slowly, but then it begins to build. The crowd is frustrated that Jesus is not who they thought he was, and they quickly join in the chant. A few people turn away shaking their heads sadly. Why is no one calling out in protest? No one is sticking up for Jesus. What harm has he really done that the people who cheered him so recently are now turning against him? An angry man standing near us says, "I heard him tell Governor Pilate that his kingdom is not of this earth. Huh. What good does that do us?"

Pilate holds up his hand. The crowd grows quiet as he says, "You know that it is a tradition for me to release one prisoner to you during the Passover celebration. I don't see that this man deserves to die, so I will grant his release for you today."

"No, release Barabbas instead," someone shouts. The chant quickly spreads throughout the crowd: "Release Barabbas instead."

Mattathias puts his arm around me and draws Honi close, when we realize what is about to happen. Then Pilate nods to the two soldiers who are standing next to Jesus, and they lead him away to his death. I don't care about Barabbas. He is a rebel and a troublemaker, and I don't want to wait around to see him released. I want to go to the temple to pray. A great sadness, a weight on my heart that I cannot explain, descends on me. I can see that the rest of my family feels the same way.

Because Honi and John Mark don't really understand what is happening and are growing restless, we take them home, give them some food, and leave them in Sarah's care. When we get to the temple, Mariam and I stop in the middle courtyard, and Mattathias and Yohanan go on into the men's court. I don't know how long we stand there praying.

"Salome, I feel as if this is a far greater tragedy than anyone realizes," Mariam whispers.

I squeeze her hand and start to notice that the sun is dim, and the day is growing dark. It does not smell like rain, but the sky is growing darker by the minute. Still, we don't want to leave yet. So, we stay and we pray.

We are waiting for Mattathias and Yohanan and wondering at the darkness when, all of a sudden, there is an ear-splitting sound like the heavens have been torn in two. Then men are running out of the inner temple area, and we see Yohanan and Mattathias do the same.

"What's happening?"

"Are you okay? What happened?"

Mattathias' eyes are wide as he says, "The curtain. You know that huge curtain that separates the inner sanctum of the temple from the people? It just ripped in half . . . by itself!"

"It was as if God ripped it from top to bottom," Yohanan exclaims. "It's split in two, just leaving God's presence exposed to everyone."

"Does this have something to do with Jesus?"

## 21:Friday Evening

Later, at home, someone knocks on our door. It is Peter, some of the other disciples, and a few of the women who travel with them. Some of them are weeping, and everyone is afraid. They are wondering if they can use the upstairs room again since the Sabbath has begun and it is too late for them to go back out to Bethany tonight. They all want to be together in their grief. Yohanan of course agrees, and Mattathias helps him set up a screen upstairs and lay down some mats where the women can sleep separated from the men. Mariam and Sarah and I take up some clean water and extra food. I'm not sure if they have even eaten.

Mariam and I are able to talk with some of the women, who tell us that around noon, Jesus and two rebels were taken out to a high spot beside the road that the Romans often use for crucifixions. It is a heavily traveled crossroad right outside of the city walls. Because it faces a cliffside where several caves' positions give the impression of a skull, it is called "Golgotha."

"Jesus had been beaten pretty badly before they even put him up on the cross," they say sadly.

"Some other man had to carry Jesus' cross bar for him for the last part of the way."

They tell us that Jesus acknowledged them and made sure that his mother would be looked after by John. In fact, John is over in the corner comforting her right now. They say that Jesus prayed to God to forgive his very executioners. "And he told one of the men, also being crucified, that he would see him in paradise this very day." These followers are obviously heartbroken and confused.

"Joseph of Arimathea was able to get Pilate to give him Jesus' body, and he and Nicodemus buried him quickly before sundown in Joseph's family's tomb," Peter tells us.

"And," one of the women adds, "there were soldiers watching them roll the stone into place. It looked like several of the soldiers were going to stay there and keep guard."

"I can't believe that he's gone," another woman says tearfully. "Thank you for allowing us to spend the Sabbath here tomorrow.

We will go back to the tomb early the following day and do a more thorough job of wrapping his body."

Mariam nods. "Of course. You are welcome here. Sarah will bring you more food tomorrow. We are so sorry for what has happened."

"Rest well," I say quietly as we leave them to their grief. I want to speak up and say that I heard Jesus predict that this would happen, but I don't, because who am I to say what they have surely heard themselves?

∞∞∞∞∞∞∞∞∞∞∞∞∞∞∞∞∞∞

## 22:Saturday

The Sabbath day, of course, is for rest and prayer. I hate to pester Sarah, but when she comes down from taking fresh water and food upstairs, I cannot resist asking what is being said. "They are despondent," she reports. "And they are a little afraid of being arrested themselves." I hadn't even thought of that and wonder how that would affect Yohanan and Mariam.

"They are questioning how he could have done and said all that he did and still end up being killed. Some of the disciples remember Jesus claiming that he would rise again, but they are discouraged that so far nothing has happened." She adds, "Your friend Peter is very dejected. He's wondering if maybe Jesus didn't plan on things getting quite so out of control."

What a sad way to end our visit with Mariam and Yohanan and precocious John Mark, but tomorrow we will have to head back to Galilee. Mattathias must go back to work. Jesus has many friends back in Galilee who will be sad to learn of his fate. Of course, Mariam and I promise to keep in better touch, and we plan to meet again next year. There is some consolation in this renewed closeness to my cousin, and although I am so disappointed by what has happened to such a good man, I am grateful for my cousin's friendship, and I'm happy that we came.

∞∞∞∞∞∞∞∞∞∞∞∞∞∞

## 23:Sunday

Mattathias wants to get an early start, so we wake up before dawn and prepare to retrace our steps on the walk back to Capernaum. I assume that Jesus' disciples are still upstairs, and I hate to leave, but we have had a good long visit with Mariam and her family. So much has happened since we started our journey. Even if things didn't end up like everyone expected, getting to walk in a group that included Jesus and his disciples was an amazing experience. I will never forget him and the things that he said. What a world it would be if everyone actually lived their lives in the manner that he taught us to live.

We are almost to the edge of town when we see some soldiers running and shouting.

"I was awake the whole time. One minute the stone was there, and the next minute it had been moved aside!"

We stop and stand there listening.

"Those women who came with spices will tell everyone that the tomb was empty, and we'll be blamed."

"How did that happen?" one of them cries. "And who were those men dressed in white? They were telling the women that Jesus has risen!"

We shrink back against the wall as they run by. They are in a panic and don't even notice us. I beg Mattathias to let us go back and see what has happened. Something momentous has happened! I can tell that he really wants to, but we must hurry home, and so, reluctantly, we move on. I will send word to Mariam and ask what has happened. Did someone steal Jesus' body? Or is it possible that he is actually alive? I can hardly contain my excitement about the possibility! Our return journey feels so much longer than it did before. We join up with a group on the outskirts of the city, and although many people are talking about Jesus being crucified, most of them seem more disappointed in him than sad. Honi walks with Mattathias and me for a good portion of the way, and we talk quietly about the soldiers who ran past us. Could something have happened that no one else knows about yet? I can't think about anything else as we start the descent back down toward the Jordan River and then north toward home.

◇◇◇◇◇◇◇◇◇◇◇◇◇◇◇◇◇◇◇◇◇◇◇◇◇◇◇◇◇◇◇◇◇

## 24:Some Time Later

Dear Salome,

Thank you for your letter. John Mark is writing this one for me. Our lives have been changed forever by what has happened in Jerusalem over the past few weeks. You asked about Jesus, and you will not believe it. He did rise from the dead. HE DID! Just like he said he would. The morning that you left us, Mary and a couple of the other women took the spices that they had prepared and went to the tomb to try and finish wrapping Jesus' body. They said that they were going to ask the soldiers there to help them roll away the stone at the entrance. But when they got there, the stone was already rolled away, and Jesus' body was not in the tomb.

The soldiers were in a panic and didn't know what had happened. Mary said that Jesus appeared to her and talked to her!

Peter and John ran to the tomb right after that and saw for themselves that it was empty. The linen clothes that Jesus had been wrapped in were lying there. I think they were still skeptical, but Peter asked Yohanan if they could continue staying upstairs until they found out for sure what had happened. That evening Jesus appeared to almost all of them upstairs. In our house, Salome! John said that Jesus just suddenly appeared in the room with them and talked to them. At first, they thought it was a ghost, but he even ate with them.

So much else has happened since then. Two of the disciples who did not stay at our house and had already left Jerusalem were walking back to Emmaus. They said that, at some point on their journey, a man began to walk with them. He explained to them that everything that had happened with Jesus was foretold in the Scriptures. They didn't recognize him at first, but they said that it turned out to be Jesus himself. Also, Thomas hadn't been there the first time that Jesus appeared to the men upstairs, but a few days later, Jesus appeared to the disciples again. He had Thomas actually touch the nail holes in his hands and the wound in his side. Now Thomas can't stop talking about it. It's amazing!

Salome, I think Jesus was actually God in the flesh! That's what John and Peter told Yohanan . . . and that it was his own kingdom that he'd been talking about. There are so many people now who say that they have seen him alive again and who believe that he is the Son of God. I really think that he IS the Messiah, in so many more ways than our people expected!

Jesus told his disciples to stay here in Jerusalem until they receive the Holy Spirit that he promised them, so they are renting the upstairs room permanently now. We have gotten to know them all well.

I wish you could be here. People all over the city are amazed. There are hundreds of us now who are determined to do what Jesus said. We are all meeting together almost every day and telling stories over and over again about what Jesus did and the stories he told. It's the most wonderful thing that has ever happened!

Actually, you may get to see for yourself. Evidently Jesus told his friends that he would meet them back up in Galilee sometime later. I hope you get to see him! What a miracle. I can't imagine that things will ever be the same. Surely, the whole world has been changed!

God's kingdom—Jesus' kingdom—is coming.

We must talk again soon.

Shalom,

Your cousin Mariam

# Daily Devotional and Reading Guide

*Your Journey: An Introduction to the Devotional Readings*

S tories like that of Salome are inspirational and thought-provoking. They allow us to envision ourselves in the shoes of those who saw and interacted with Jesus. As you read through the narrative of Salome and her family, you will see a glimpse into possible experiences of the unnamed and otherwise unknown bystanders who would have seen Jesus and experienced his ministry.

The purpose of this devotional is to add a companion piece to Salome's journey, providing scriptural, cultural, and historical context to her story. Each day of their journey, as you read through this devotional, I hope you'll take time with the scripture first and then the accompanying commentary. Each daily meditation is designed to provoke additional feelings and thoughts about the story being told. Whether you read the story first and then engage in a time of devotion or whether you read both simultaneously, we hope that this section will provide a meditative companion to the narrative that will help you personalize the story for your own life and journey.

As you embark upon this excursion with us (and with Salome and Mattathias), we hope you will feel the impulse to share this story with others, even as you experience for yourself all of the hope and joy found in the promise of our Lord and Savior.

As I prepared to write this devotional, I thought of Psalm 78. Psalm 78 provides a brilliant lesson for us about the importance of story in our lives and of passing on our faith to younger generations. This story is both a personal journey and a relational one, a story that highlights both hope and responsibility—responsibility in the sense that we are called to teach those who come after us and hope in the sense that we know if we do so, this earth will be filled with the love and grace of the God who created us.

Today, think of your own family. What did the previous generations instill in you? Why do they matter to you today? Spend some time reflecting on future generations and the ways you care for them. What are the lessons and traditions you hope to pass along to them, and how can you do that during your time together?

This devotional is designed to be used at any time of year. You can read the selections that accompany the journey by journal date, or you can read the entries by scripture notation (for the forty days of Lent). Whichever way you choose to read with us, we hope that your soul will be nourished and your spirit refreshed by this wonderful and amazing story of Jesus and his companions.

Rev. Jimmy Decker

# 1: Tuesday Afternoon

*Lent One: Isaiah 58:6-9*

The start of every season is truly the start of a journey. But Lent for us is especially vital. It is the beginning of a season in which we point our eyes toward the cross and identify our own mortality. Just as we see Salome and her family prepare for this journey, there's a bit of uncertainty each year as we approach Ash Wednesday. We ready our hearts and minds for a conversation about what we have, what we need to leave behind, and what we need to receive. In the history of the Church, the season of Lent has been marked as one in which we are willing to give up something, with the start of a fast that begins with Ash Wednesday and concludes on Easter Sunday. As we look to the Old Testament prophets, we see encouragement that shows what fasting ought to look like. More importantly, we see instruction for how we can fast in such a way as to actually live into the faithful life that is God's will for us. All too often, we think about fasting as a diet of sorts, literally giving up chocolate or soda. Yet the best way to fast is to be willing to leave behind the things that prevent us from living faithfully and take up the articles we need for the journey to care for those around us and to love God and neighbor more fully.

This Ash Wednesday, challenge yourself to think through what it might mean for you to fast. Perhaps this is a practice you have engaged in every year, or maybe this is something you are doing for the first time. Pray over the words of Isaiah. See what you need for a journey with Christ and what you can leave behind. Then ask yourself what would be necessary to more fully live into a grace-filled love for the world around you. Challenge yourself to give up the very thing this season that might prevent you from fully loving God and others. Embark on a faith walk with Christ through this story and, more importantly, through the story of the gospel.

If you are embarking on this journey in a different season, think about creating your own journal entries to chart your insights and encounters with Jesus, just as Salome did. How do you see Jesus appearing in your own life? What about his healings and teachings surprise you? How is he changing the way you think about the world, your faith, and your life?

## *Lent Two: Matthew 3:1-6*

As Salome speaks with Mattathias, we see them reference a story about Jesus' baptism and the man who baptized him, John. John was a wild man to say the least, but he was called to be an emissary for Christ. What is beautiful about John's story is that he didn't think any more of his calling or who he was than he ought to, but instead maintained a sense of humility. He fully recognized that he was called to announce the Messiah's arrival. While he baptized people, he affirmed that it was not he who was providing any grace or salvation. Rather, these would come through Christ. God invites us to see our roles in life in this same way. We are called not to save anyone else but instead simply to tell the story of who Jesus is and the work he is doing in this world. Frankly, this sort of reimagining of our roles in the story of God's work can be freeing. It isn't up to us to bring others to Christ, but instead we offer the truth of Christ's love to them and leave the rest up to God. We get to be wingmen and women who simply introduce others to God. While this may seem daunting, we find an example of how we can talk about Jesus from Salome and Mattathias. We can speak not only about his authority and good works but also about his kindness and care. Truly each of us can find some comfort in hearing about a person who is powerful, yet gentle, and who came to offer us a life of love and joy regardless of our circumstances.

Today, think about how you can spread the message of Christ to others you encounter. Perhaps you can do so through your words, engaging in a helpful conversation with a friend in need and reminding him or her of the hope of Jesus. Or perhaps your actions can speak louder than those words in offering that same love and care that Jesus offered to a stranger. Today, be like John and announce Jesus to the world.

# My Journal

....................................................................................................
....................................................................................................
....................................................................................................
....................................................................................................
....................................................................................................
....................................................................................................
....................................................................................................
....................................................................................................
....................................................................................................
....................................................................................................
....................................................................................................
....................................................................................................
....................................................................................................
....................................................................................................
....................................................................................................
....................................................................................................
....................................................................................................
....................................................................................................

# 2: Tuesday Evening

## *Lent Three: Romans 12:16-21*

As we see Salome describe her life, we see a small glimpse into the daily life of a typical family in the first century. Lives were marked with humility but also pride in the joy that was found in this simple way of living. The incredible part of the story about Salome and her family emerges with the reality that the Jesus they keep hearing about came for people just like them. In that day and age, it was the common belief that the deck was stacked in favor of those who were wealthy and powerful. And yet Christ would begin a revolution that focused on caring for and loving people of every status. We too are encouraged to live this same mentality, not persecuting or turning away from anyone in need but instead being good stewards and neighbors to those around us, people from every walk of life. Later in the New Testament, Paul would give this same sort of encouragement to the church in Rome. He explained that we ought to live for joy and harmony rather than living for vengeance and hostility. While we mostly believe this is the life we want to live, our actions don't always reflect that. Salome's story, today's Scripture, and most importantly Jesus' ministry encourage us to find a harmonious way of living with our neighbors and community.

Today, take a moment to give thanks to God for all that you have. Pray a prayer of humility and gratitude, identifying one specific way in which you have been blessed. Then take a moment to reflect on how you can use that blessing to bless others around you. Invite someone over for a meal, do a task for someone out of kindness, or perhaps strike up a conversation with someone who seems alone. All of these are ways for us to live out the message of Christ.

# My Journal

....................................................................................

....................................................................................

....................................................................................

....................................................................................

....................................................................................

....................................................................................

....................................................................................

....................................................................................

....................................................................................

....................................................................................

....................................................................................

....................................................................................

....................................................................................

....................................................................................

....................................................................................

....................................................................................

....................................................................................

....................................................................................

# 3: Wednesday Morning

*Lent Four: Psalm 34:17-18*

We have no record of Jesus approaching Salome in Scripture. But while the story of Salome is fictional, it is deeply rooted in the truths of the gospel. The actions and words of Jesus in this moment, offering peace and comfort to one in grief, serve as inspiration and encouragement for all of us. Jesus came into this world as God incarnate, God fully taking on the flesh and the weaknesses of humanity. As a result, we know that Christ experienced hardship, sadness, and grief himself. The joy in this truth is that we worship a God who knows what we are going through. As the old saying goes, "misery loves company." We have seen this as a phrase which implies that those who are hurting will bring others into that pain. When we are in pain, it is helpful to know that someone else understands. The joy of the gospel is knowing that Christ on the cross experienced all that pain and suffering, so that in our saddest moments, we can look to him and realize we are not alone in our pain. This assurance can bring us a sense of hope.

Today, try to identify someone in your life who is going through a hard time. Work to genuinely empathize with that pain and struggle. Perhaps you know someone who recently experienced the loss of a job or the death of a loved one. Take a moment to engage with them, not trying to take away their pain but offering them the assurance of relationship and love that Christ offers each of us.

## *Lent Five: Matthew 8:23-27; Matthew 14:22-33; Mark 5:35-43; Mark 6:30-44*

Today, we hear Salome recounting three different miracles that Jesus performed, each of them as awe-inspiring as the last. In the original Greek, we understand miracle to translate roughly as a "sign of wonder." These days, someone would see or hear about a sign of wonder and immediately dismiss it as fake. News outlets would run stories about the man who walked on water, chuckling as they report about the witnesses needing to have their eyes checked. We have a great amount of skepticism baked into our culture as a result of social media and the advancements of technology. This viewpoint diminishes our ability to be amazed and to have greater faith. We should obviously not believe every story we hear, but perhaps we should not be so dismissive of the possibility of miracles. While we may never see a man walk on water, we have seen miracles occur in medicine, in relationships, and in just about every other walk of life. When we see marriages mended after periods of strife, see children accomplish some truly incredible feat after great determination, or see someone healed in ways that aren't understood by medicine, we can take heart in the reality that miracles continue to happen to this day. Buying into the possibility of miracles actually allows us to believe in what God is truly capable of, even now.

Today, take a moment to pray to God. Thank God for some miracle that you have experienced in your life. If you cannot think of one, thank God for the reality that miracles do happen, and ask for the wisdom and the openness to see them as they occur. Then encourage yourself to embrace what is possible in Christ the next time you see your own sign of wonder.

∞∞∞∞∞∞∞∞∞∞∞∞∞∞∞∞∞∞∞∞∞∞∞∞∞∞∞∞∞∞∞∞∞∞∞∞∞∞∞∞∞∞∞∞∞∞

## *Lent Six: Genesis 1:31*

The world around us is a reminder of the glory of God. This sentiment is often casually repeated in a variety of ways, but usually we don't realize just how true it is. When we look around at the world, we see constant reminders of the goodness of God. God created the world and, upon doing so, called it good. God created humanity and called us very good. Therefore, as we look around the world, we can see the goodness of that world and find peace and joy in the fact that we are surrounded by examples of the goodness of God. Salome shows us that there is goodness all around us in the form of both the earth and the people and creatures who inhabit it. God created all of this for good, and while there have been moments where the brokenness of the world has made an appearance, we can take solace in knowing that the goodness of God's creation is unyielding. The only thing stopping us from living into this goodness is us. If we, like Salome, begin to see the beauty around us and the ways in which we have been blessed, we will see how our blessings are a calling for us to go out and be the blessing for others. Put simply, we are blessed to be a blessing.

Take a moment to be like Salome in this excerpt of the story. Take five minutes today to pause at work or at home. Reflect on all that is around you, both in people and in nature. In what ways are they good? In what ways are they blessings to you and your life? As you reflect on these blessings, ask yourself this: for whom have I been called to be a blessing? Identify some steps that you can take to be a blessing to others today.

# My Journal

........................................................................................
........................................................................................
........................................................................................
........................................................................................
........................................................................................
........................................................................................
........................................................................................
........................................................................................
........................................................................................
........................................................................................
........................................................................................
........................................................................................
........................................................................................
........................................................................................
........................................................................................
........................................................................................
........................................................................................
........................................................................................
........................................................................................

# 4: Wednesday Afternoon

*Lent Seven: Daniel 7:13-14*

A prevalent theme throughout the New Testament speaks to how the Israelite people were waiting many years for a Messiah. The Israelite people were often oppressed by other kingdoms and rulers and clung to the hope that one day they would receive salvation through a messiah figure who would be their savior. As Jesus' followers walked along beside him toward the cross, they would have begun to see that their vision of a savior, a great warrior who would ride in on a powerful horse to save the day and become their earthly king, was off base. Jesus would be their savior, but this salvation would take place not in an earthly manner but on an eternal, cosmic scale instead. Looking at the Scripture passage from Daniel, we see a vision of the Son of Man. This vision is something that would be fulfilled by Christ through his life, death, and resurrection. Jesus himself claimed to be the fulfillment of Daniel's prophecy (Mark 14:62). Today, Christ continues to subvert the expectations of the world. To live more fully into our faith, we must be willing to think outside of the box. Jesus turned the world upside down. True power comes from humility and selflessness rather than from force and a self-centered mindset. The challenge for us is to recognize not only that this same framework of salvation is available to us today, but that we are challenged to actively accept that grace and salvation each day.

Take an opportunity to recognize how Christ would challenge the status quo in the world around you today. Is there a way to lower yourself and live more humbly either in your workplace or in your personal life? What would it mean for your faith if you did so? Would that change the response you have to what is happening in our world right now? Is there an example of Christ's behavior that you can live out today through your words and actions?

## *Lent Eight: Galatians 3:23-28*

This story of Salome is an encouraging vision of how the world worked, how the world might still work today for some, and how we might live into the kingdom of God more fully. In biblical days, there were clear societal norms about the roles of men and women. Jesus challenged these norms on a regular basis, creating a sense of levelness between men and women. We see examples throughout Scripture in which Jesus found those who were considered "less than" in society and elevated them to a venerated status among their people. This holds true for the way that he engaged with women, as well as those who were sick, those who were orphaned, and those who were despised in society. Paul echoes this sentiment in his letter to the Galatians, making it clear that in Christ there is no male or female, Jew or Greek, slave or free. Jesus' vision for the kingdom of God asserts a genuine adoration for the uniqueness of each person, while also holding strong to the idea that each person is of equal worth and standing. In engaging with this idea that we are one united people under Christ, we move closer to the original vision for the world that God had upon creating it: people whose love supersedes persecution and rejection.

Today, identify someone in your life who might feel as though he or she is not considered of equal worth. Perhaps it is a woman in a field dominated by men. Perhaps it is a child who feels like he or she is not loved or respected. Perhaps it is a coworker who thinks he or she stands on a lower level than you. Ask yourself how God is calling you to love and respect those people in the way that Jesus would. What specifically can you do to show them that the kingdom of God is one in which no person is held in higher regard than another?

## *Lent Nine: Luke 10:25-37*

The dispute between the Jews and the Samaritans was a constant rivalry that had grown into a deep-seated hatred for one another. It is not unrealistic to think people like Salome and her family would have been raised to never associate or interact with the Samaritans. Even those Jews who were inspired by the radical message of community and love that Jesus was teaching still had a belief that the Samaritans ought to be despised. This was notably seen when two disciples were rejected by a Samaritan village and they wanted to call down fire upon the villagers, only to be stopped by Jesus. In this way, we come to see that there are always animosities that we hold as humans for people who are different than we are. The teachings of Jesus would have us look at how those people are loved and redeemed by Christ just as we are, and as a result have an equal capacity for goodness. In no place is this better summed up than in the message of the good Samaritan.

Jesus upends the thinking of the people around him by making a despised Samaritan the hero of a parable. This subversion of expectations is important for us to remember in our daily lives, because we are called not only to be good Samaritans for others but also to recognize the good Samaritans around us.

Today, take an opportunity to think about someone who has wronged you in the past or someone you are at odds with over some disagreement. How would Christ encourage you to interact with that person today? If the kingdom of God is a place where we are all truly equal, then how can we reconcile with the people whom we previously have seen as outcasts or "less than" in society? What have you done to accomplish that?

## *Lent Ten: Luke 17:11-19*

This passage serves to demonstrate Jesus' heavenly abilities. We not only see a sign of wonder, but we also see Jesus' ability to restore the outcasts to a place in society, and to articulate (albeit discreetly) his identity as God. In this time period, lepers were cast out of the places where people lived, out of fear that they would spread their illness to others. They were unable to hide that they had this disease either, as it resulted in sores, rashes, and other deformities. Jesus heals ten lepers, and after they realize what has happened, they vocally praised God because they can now return to living among, and having relationships, with other people! At the end of the passage of Scripture, one of the men returns to Jesus to worship him for this healing. Jesus asks him where the other men are and praises him for not only accepting the gift of healing that was offered but also recognizing who offered the gift in the first place. His faith is celebrated as a result, and he is encouraged to go forth, because it is his faith that has made him well. Jesus creates a distinction between physical and spiritual healing. While some were physically healed, this man was healed in his soul because he recognized the person of Jesus. As we traverse life, it is easy to celebrate the blessings we receive while forgetting to give thanks to God, who gave us those blessings in the first place.

Today, thank God for some blessing that you have received recently. Acknowledge that this blessing is from God. Do your best to sit in an attitude of gratitude and thanksgiving, simply offering these up to God. Ask God where you are to go next, knowing that it is through your faith that you will be encouraged to go forth and continue to be a servant of Christ.

# My Journal

................................................................................
................................................................................
................................................................................
................................................................................
................................................................................
................................................................................
................................................................................
................................................................................
................................................................................
................................................................................
................................................................................
................................................................................
................................................................................
................................................................................
................................................................................
................................................................................
................................................................................
................................................................................
................................................................................
................................................................................

# 5: Wednesday Evening

*Lent Eleven: Matthew 19:16-26*

Salome's story ascribes a name and some background to the rich young man who approaches Jesus. This man hopes that he will be told he has done enough to enter heaven because he has lived a life by the law, yet Jesus once again subverts expectations. Rather than celebrating the work the man has already done, Jesus challenges him to think through how much more he can do. It is no longer about doing everything according to the letter of the law, but instead about asking ourselves how far we are willing to go. In terms of giving, it is not about giving what makes us comfortable, but about giving what's uncomfortable. In terms of time, it's about asking ourselves if we're willing to prioritize our faith as a part of our calendar.

This story is interesting because many see it ending with the man walking away, sad upon hearing that he must sell his possessions to enter heaven. Many people interpret the story to mean that this man will not enter heaven, because he is unwilling to part with his possessions and wealth. Truthfully, we do not know how this man's story ends. Perhaps he ends up rejecting Jesus' teaching, or perhaps he decides at some point to fully commit and actually sell all that he has. The encouragement for us is to realize that entrance to heaven is a greater prize in and of itself than anything that is in front of us, greater than anything that we can own or achieve! And it's never too late to take the actions necessary to prioritize God.

Today, identify something you are willing to sacrifice in order to grow closer to Jesus. If prioritizing your schedule is your issue, make time in your calendar to make this happen. If it is money or possessions, commit today to be willing to give those things up in the hopes that doing so will open your eyes a bit wider and point them to Christ. While these things are not easy to do, we can find hope in knowing that Christ sees this struggle in us and is offering us encouragement and strength to follow through.

## *Lent Twelve: Matthew 20:1-16*

Wanting fair compensation for our work is something that is understandable, and frankly, right. If we do a day's worth of work, we deserve pay that equals that time and effort. If we do half a day of work, we deserve less than we would deserve if we did a full day's worth. This mentality is, for most people, not something that is up for debate. For this reason, this is one of the most difficult parables for us to accept in a modern context. The purpose of Jesus' story is to help direct our faith away from the work that we have done and instead direct it toward the gift that God is offering. If we see salvation as something that is to be earned, then the amount of work that we put into it matters. But if we see salvation as something that is a gift, then it is not about the work we've done. It is about the person offering the gift in the first place. Think of it in the context of love. While you may be the oldest child of your parents, you don't deserve more love than a younger sibling simply because you've been a part of the family longer. Each new sibling introduced should receive the same amount of love that you have received from your parents. Love should be equally given . . . and with God, it is!

Today, identify someone in your life whom you think "doesn't deserve" something they've been given. Ask yourself if they truly don't deserve it, or if it is just difficult to accept that what they received is not something they earned. After identifying this, take an opportunity to go celebrate that with them. You will hopefully find that the joy of celebration is a far greater state of mind than that of jealousy and disdain.

## *Lent Thirteen: Mark 2:23-28*

Taking time to rest is difficult. We live in a hectic world with a great number of demands on our time. Weekends and days off immediately become filled with appointments and chores that we didn't get to during the week. The Sabbath is a tradition deeply rooted in Jewish faith. Since the beginning of creation, it has been deemed that one ought to take some time for rest. In the Genesis creation narrative, it says that God rested after creating all that we see around us. In the Old Testament, God then invited the Israelites to participate in this same practice, and their people continued doing so well into the time of Jesus' ministry. Unfortunately, the concept of Sabbath would eventually become misconstrued, and the Jewish leaders would use this to vilify and condemn Jesus. The command to do no work on the Sabbath would become legalistic and restrictive, rather than a spiritual practice intended to strengthen our souls.

We ought to remember that preparing for, and subsequently taking, Sabbath allows us to take inventory of the priorities in our lives: our faith, our family, our community. Sabbath is meant to be enriching and not only helps us to recuperate from the days before, but also prepares us for the days ahead. It provides opportunity to reflect and become creative. It allows for deeper relationships with the people around us. Sabbath was not made by God to ensure that one day a week everyone would stop and worship God. Sabbath was a gift from God to us so that we could experience a fuller life. Jesus understood that and taught this accordingly in Scripture.

Take some time to identify what Sabbath will be for you this week. Perhaps you can have a genuine Sabbath on Sunday, but perhaps not. Perhaps you already have preexisting commitments or your work requires you to be "on" this weekend. In that case, find a day with some meaningful period of time in it when you can spend time with God and the people you love. Use it to be refilled and recharged by God for the work you've already done, and the work you still have ahead.

# My Journal

..........................................................................................................................

..........................................................................................................................

..........................................................................................................................

..........................................................................................................................

..........................................................................................................................

..........................................................................................................................

..........................................................................................................................

..........................................................................................................................

..........................................................................................................................

..........................................................................................................................

..........................................................................................................................

..........................................................................................................................

..........................................................................................................................

..........................................................................................................................

..........................................................................................................................

..........................................................................................................................

..........................................................................................................................

..........................................................................................................................

..........................................................................................................................

# 6: Thursday Morning

*Lent Fourteen: Mark 10:32-34*

On at least three occasions in each of the Gospels, Jesus takes an opportunity to predict his death to his disciples and followers. The goal of this is to begin to set the stage for them to see how the words of the prophets of the Old Testament would be fulfilled in him as the Christ, and to understand that salvation is coming. Each time, however, the disciples either choose to brush off this warning or refuse to accept it for what it is and become angry at the proposition. In this same way, we see Salome aghast at the idea that Jesus would be put to death for his works and teaching, but more importantly, that death is something which could ever be conquered. Ancient Israelite culture didn't believe that death was something to overcome, and so the idea that Jesus could be greater than death would sound ridiculous, and the implication of it (that Jesus could actually be God) was even more preposterous.

Even with these forewarnings, Jesus knew that his death would come as an incredible shock to his followers, because they believed that he was going to be the next great revolutionary leader for the Israelites. From a theological perspective, we see Salome uncover a truth here, which is that Jesus was aware of the work that needed to be done and still chose to move forward with it. This demonstrates God's love for us in that, when all was dire in front of him, Jesus persevered for our sake. In this way, we ought to take comfort in the truth that Jesus was willing to go to the cross not just for the people with whom he interacted two millennia ago, but for the people who live today as well. It was this love for each person who walks this earth that made Jesus determined to see his mission to fulfillment.

Take a moment to reflect on your own worth. As we grow in our faith, we come to see that although we are broken and flawed, sinful and imperfect, Christ deems us worthy. Christ's decision to go to the cross and experience death for us is a result of Christ deciding that we were worth saving. For this reason, accept that you have been made worthy in the eyes of God, and more importantly, so too have the people around you.

## Lent Fifteen: Luke 5:17-26

In one of the more famous passages of scripture, we see Jesus' healing of a man who is lowered through a roof by his friends. In performing this healing, Jesus experiences some of his first opposition from the religious leaders who call his teachings blasphemy because he claims to forgive sins (only God can do that!). Jesus addresses this idea that "anyone could say your sins are forgiven because it can't be verified" by performing a miracle that is instantly verified with a man getting up and walking. While there are deep theological truths to unpack in this act of Jesus to both heal the man and prove his divinity in front of the Pharisees, this passage also offers many practical applications. One of the more important ones is the difference between physical and spiritual healing. While it is nice for this man to get up and walk, what he truly needs from Jesus is spiritual restoration. The faith of this man, along with the faith of his friends, is what allows him to experience that spiritual (and physical) healing when he is lowered down through a roof into the room with Jesus. As we navigate life, we recognize that there are friends around us who need us to lower them down into the room with Jesus. In the same way, there are friends we depend on to lower us down as well. It is faith in Christ, as well as dependence on one another, that allows us to experience life to its fullest.

Think through the friends in your life. Is there someone around you who needs healing in an emotional or spiritual sense? Take a moment to listen to God about how you might be the one to offer and encourage that spiritual healing. What healing do you need from God and others? Who makes up the community around you and who would be there to help if you were willing to reach out and ask? Today, ask God for the courage to go forth and ask your friends for this support and care as you pursue this healing for yourself in the same way.

## Lent Sixteen: 1 Samuel 16:4-13

If you have ever had a child, you know the woes of comparison. Between parenting books, pediatrician milestones, and the internet, it is easy to compare your child to every other baby in existence, both the actual and the hypothetical. Is your son or daughter in the greatest height/weight percentages, and are they reaching milestones ahead of the curve? The issue with this mentality is that it inherently robs you of time to simply enjoy your child for who he or she is. Perhaps you don't know this feeling, but you surely know what it's like to compare yourself to a neighbor or friend who has more than you. The same issue still persists:

comparison is the thief of joy. The idea of comparing ourselves to others is not a new phenomenon of the twenty-first century. Since the beginning of time, we humans have compared ourselves to others. Yet this is antithetical to the story of God. In the story of David being chosen as king, notice that he was the youngest and smallest of the family. By human standards, he shouldn't have been the one chosen. By every comparative metric, he should have been last. Yet God measures the qualities of the heart. What Salome is soon to find is that while she may not have as much as her cousin, the gospel truth and the promises of Jesus are available to her as well. She has as much value and worth in the eyes of God as her cousin. In this same way, we have as much value and worth as anyone else we see, because God measures our worth on a different scale.

Today, you have the opportunity to see worth in the same way as God. You have the opportunity to impact someone in a positive way and to help them feel valued and loved. Compliment someone in a meaningful way. Perhaps that person is wearing something nice or did good work on a project recently. Be a force for God by showing that friend or acquaintance that not only does God see his or her worth, but other humans do as well.

# My Journal

# 7: Thursday Afternoon

*Lent Seventeen: Matthew 4:18-22*

As Salome journeys alongside Jesus, she is in an interesting place where she understands the threat that Jesus seems to pose to the power of the religious leaders and to the norms of Israelite culture, and yet she doesn't seem to think that he is doing anything wrong. The message Jesus is teaching resonates with her and so many others, and for this reason she believes in the goodness of his work. This is aided by the fact that the disciples whom Jesus surrounds himself with are people much like her and her family. They are simple men in working-class jobs. They are flawed beings, and yet they are passionately following Christ after each receiving a calling from Jesus to do so. What Salome doesn't necessarily recognize is that this is a constant theme in the way in which God operates. Often it is the people who are least expected to succeed who are the ones called by God to lead for the Kingdom. The most prominent example of this is when David was selected to be king, despite being the youngest son of Jesse. From Old Testament to New Testament, God uses people whom we ourselves wouldn't choose to be vessels of God's work. In this way, we are challenged to hear how God is calling us despite our own brokenness and our own flaws. Each one of us is called to live out our faith in spite of our weaknesses. The disciples would carry this lesson with them into the Book of Acts and the beginnings of the church. It was a lesson that would remain as an essential part of our Christian faith to this day.

How has God called you? How has God called the people around you? You might think you are better than they are. You might think they are better than you. Regardless, each of us has the privilege to be a disciple for God. What unique gifts, life experiences, or expertise do you have that could benefit the lives of others for the glory of God? Take some time today to reflect on and identify something you can do for the church or for your community.

## *Lent Eighteen: John 14:5-7; Mark 10:35-45; Philippians 2:5-11*

We live in a culture and mentality where we want to be "the best" in every aspect of our lives. We are constantly comparing ourselves to others and determining ways in which we can get a leg up and ascend to greater heights as a result. This is true in education and business, in public and private sectors; it is true with accomplishments as well as with possessions. Our society (and maybe our innate desire) pushes us to compete and to compare. When Jesus hears his own disciples lean into this mentality, he quickly puts them in their place. They want to jockey for positions of power within the kingdom of heaven, but Jesus reminds them that this is not the way his kingdom works. He says that for people to truly be exalted, they must humble themselves and become servants of their fellow humans. God has chosen to use us flawed human beings to help bring about God's kingdom on earth. It is only with humility that we can participate fully and joyfully in God's work while growing into the people that God calls us to be.

What are you good at? Take some time to be honest with yourself today about the gifts that you have. Then ask God to humble you and to give you the heart of a lowly servant. Ask that God inspire you to see that you have wonderful gifts and that you are called to humbly use those gifts for God's kingdom, not to lift yourself up to greatness or power or fame.

## *Lent Nineteen: Luke 18:35-43*

Have you ever wanted something so badly in life that you dreamt of what it would look like before you ever had it? How many times when you've done this have you ended up being disappointed in it when it arrived? Was the gift itself actually disappointing? Or had you just created an incorrect image of it in your head? In this story, we see a stark contrast between the disciples' desires and Jesus' actions. The disciples and the Jewish community had been looking for a Messiah, someone to rescue them from the watchful rule of the Roman leaders as well as from the persecutory Pharisees. Jesus' followers believed him to be this Messiah, this revolutionary leader. What Salome sees in this story is the disciples expecting Jesus to be the version of the Messiah they've always dreamt of. They think he is too busy and important to have time for individual needs like healing a blind man. Jesus' action in this moment is as much for the disciples as it is for the blind man: he heals Bartimaeus to demonstrate his spiritual ability, but also to show his disciples that he has come to be the savior of individuals as well as of the world. He has been setting the stage for them to see that he is not going to be the Messiah they have dreamt up in their heads, but that he will be a Messiah who is actually far greater. Sometimes the greatest gifts imaginable come in the most unlikely of packages. Even better, sometimes those gifts are beyond what we were even asking for in the first place. Jesus does not disappoint in the end!

Who is the one blind beggar you can care for today? You likely won't encounter a sightless man on the streets as Jesus did. There is, however, one person you will encounter today that you can take the time to lift up with God's love. Maybe it's a coworker having a bad day. Maybe it's a neighbor who needs help with a chore. Maybe it's a stranger in the grocery store whom you can simply give a Starbucks gift card to for no reason—other than spreading God's love. Take the time to do something. Do something today. For at least one person.

# My Journal

........................................................................................

........................................................................................

........................................................................................

........................................................................................

........................................................................................

........................................................................................

........................................................................................

........................................................................................

........................................................................................

........................................................................................

........................................................................................

........................................................................................

........................................................................................

........................................................................................

........................................................................................

........................................................................................

........................................................................................

........................................................................................

........................................................................................

........................................................................................

........................................................................................

# 8: Friday Morning

*Lent Twenty: Luke 19:1-10*

This story of Zacchaeus seems like almost an afterthought for Salome as she recounts it, particularly as she doesn't witness it firsthand, but it is truly one of the most profound and important stories in Scripture surrounding Jesus' ministry. In those days, a tax collector was a supremely reviled being. Tax collectors had the responsibility of gathering the taxes from the people, yet there was no oversight or procedure that governed this practice. Thus, a tax collector's wages would mostly come from his ability to overtax the citizens and to keep the surplus for himself. The tax collectors basically stole the livelihood of the very communities in which they lived! Couple with this the fact that they worked for the Roman government, whose taxes they collected. This marked them as traitors to their own people. Put simply, they were nobody's friend. For Jesus not only to engage with a tax collector, Zacchaeus, but also to dine with him was a massive upheaval in societal norms. It's one of the more monumental moments in Jesus' ministry. It demonstrates our calling not to discount someone based upon society's perception, but instead to see others in the way that Christ would see them. The reason Jesus was so willing to dine with Zacchaeus was not necessarily to make a point, though a point was in fact made, but instead to simply care for someone who was a child of God. Our perceptions of others often clash with God's perceptions. In this way, we can fail to value others the way that God calls us to.

This world is deeply divided on so many issues due to current events, social media, and politics. As a result, we have created lines of division that cause us to see others as proverbial Zacchaeuses in our own lives. The challenge for us is to recognize how we are seeing them in this way, and then to react to them differently. Can you identify someone in your life with whom you have a deep-seated disagreement? How would God have you engage with them today as opposed to how you would have engaged with them in the past?

## Lent Twenty-One: Matthew 25:14-30; 1 Timothy 6:17-19

The parable of the talents is an interesting one that has had many interpretations. The obvious message is that God is asking us to be like the first two servants, to go forth and use what God has given us to create further good. Multiply what blessings you have into more blessings (specifically for others)! A talent was a measure of currency. There is some debate about its exact value, but it was a large amount, maybe even twenty years' worth of wages. Jesus is referencing significant amounts of money. He's not simply talking about $5 bills. With that in mind, it becomes a little more understandable that the third servant would choose not to do anything with the talent. He had some level of fear that all of this money could be lost. So he didn't take any risk with it. As a result, he was able to safely return the exact amount to his master. However, the parable makes it clear that this is not satisfying to God. This sort of "safe play" meant that it was impossible to use what he had been given to accomplish anything good. Instead, Jesus says that those who take what they have been given and attempt to multiply it for the Kingdom will be rewarded. An interesting thought exercise would be to ask, "What if one of the servants had made a valiant attempt to grow his talents but had been unsuccessful and returned with less than he had been given? Would he still be rewarded and blessed by God?" The parable seems to indicate that yes, he would. It was less about the profit that the servants had gained and more about the effort that they had made. The parable seems to indicate that by putting in the work, by making an attempt to use wisely what God has given us, this makes it inevitable that God will help double our efforts for good! Regardless of interpretation, the basic message is clear: we are called to do more than sit idly by as the kingdom of God unfolds.

What have you been given? What blessings do you have? Time? Money? Health? Education? Access to power or influence? Relationships? Many of us think that we haven't been blessed, when each of us has access to something that we can leverage for God's work in this world. The question is whether we're willing to do it. If we remove our fear that we are somehow responsible for the "multiplication" of those gifts and remember that God is simply looking for effort from us, we can remember that God will "take it from here." God has given us the chance to participate. . . . in fact, God requires it. Pray today about how you can use your talents for the kingdom of God.

# My Journal

...........................................................................

...........................................................................

...........................................................................

...........................................................................

...........................................................................

...........................................................................

...........................................................................

...........................................................................

...........................................................................

...........................................................................

...........................................................................

...........................................................................

...........................................................................

...........................................................................

...........................................................................

...........................................................................

...........................................................................

...........................................................................

# 9:Friday Afternoon

*Lent Twenty-Two: Matthew 16:21-28*

As we continue the story of Salome, there's a bit of dramatic irony that is occurring. We know that Jesus and those around him are barreling toward sacrifice. We have already seen Jesus give notice to his disciples that one day he will be taken from them. What they fail to realize is that he will be willing to sacrifice himself for humanity when that day comes. This dramatic irony is important for us to reflect on as the audience of both this story and of Scripture. We know where it's heading. We ought to read the words of Jesus understanding that he knows where the story is heading. There has been much debate for over two thousand years about the implications of Jesus' sacrifice. What we know is that this sacrifice changed everything for us! God used the Israelites' concept of animal sacrifice (where sins were atoned for and right relationship with God was restored) and substituted himself, in the form of Jesus, as the ultimate sacrifice which would restore to him all of humankind forever. Sacrifice of animals was no longer needed. Instead, sacrifice was asked of us in return, not a literal sacrifice of our physical body, but an emotional and spiritual sacrifice. God gave everything for us, so that we can live different lives. We leave behind our old way of life in order to experience the greater joy that comes with life in Christ. The season of Lent, the concept of reflection on self, is steeped in the idea of us asking what it is that we're willing to part with as we walk through the story with Jesus, who was willing to part with everything.

Today, is there something that you are holding on to that you know you do not need? Are you willing to leave it behind for something greater? Take heart in knowing that God understands the thing that you don't want to give up. God did not want to sacrifice everything, but Jesus did it, so that we might live with him for eternity. Ask God to give you the courage and the strength to give that one thing up today.

## *Lent Twenty-Three: Joshua 3:5*

We all have moments in our lives that we dread. One of the most universal is a conversation that we do not want to have with someone close to us about something difficult. These are the conversations we fear, because they leave us feeling vulnerable. We have anything but eager anticipation in that moment. The "anticipation" of Lent is not usually talked about. We think of anticipation when it comes to Advent or at Christmas time, as we eagerly look forward to Jesus' birth. Lent is more complicated. What are we looking forward to? There's Jesus' resurrection, of course, which is wonderful. But to get there, we have to walk through Jesus' arrest and death. It is hard to claim that we excitedly anticipate those difficult moments of Jesus' death. Yet anticipation is the right word, because we are moving toward something great and grace-filled and loving. Difficulty lies ahead of us. We don't need to gloss over that and pretend it won't happen or that it isn't hard. But there is something supernatural and amazing at work! Keeping our eyes on the reality of the resurrection allows us to identify with the emotions that Salome currently has, the emotions of what "could be" and what "will be." It allows us to have anticipation. Those conversations with the people in our lives that we dread are so difficult for us only because we take our eyes off the promise that comes afterward. Those conversations become less fearsome when we remember that goodness is promised on the other side of the hardship.

There is goodness ahead of each of us, but you may need to face something you fear in order to reach that goodness, perhaps a conversation you've been dreading with a family member or friend. Take some time to pray to God and hear the hope for what lies on the other side of that difficulty. Ask God to remind you of Jesus' promise of love and restored relationship. Then ask God for the inspiration to keep your eyes fixed on that moment rather than the moment you've been dreading. Ask God to help you feel a sense of anticipation for what will be. Then ask God to give you the courage to broach the hard conversation and to push through to the goodness.

## *Lent Twenty-Four: John 11:1-44*

The story of Jesus and Lazarus is one of the most important and famous moments in Scripture. While Salome doesn't witness it herself, the reverberations of Lazarus being brought back from the dead do not escape her. The implications of such a story are incredible. If Jesus could truly bring a man back from the dead, then there's really nothing that can't be done. It is important to note here that Lazarus' story differs from Jesus' resurrection in that Lazarus would eventually die again. He is not still alive, whereas Jesus was raised from the dead and remains alive. Jesus was resurrected; Lazarus was resuscitated. Jesus conquered death once and for all. That theological distinction aside, the story is also notable in that it demonstrates Jesus' divine understanding. When those around him were distraught at Lazarus' condition prior to death, Jesus reassures them by saying that the illness "will not end in death," a statement made true by the fact that Lazarus' story did not end there. It also shows Jesus' humanity as he wept. God incarnate experienced such deep sadness and emotion that he was moved to tears, and he wept openly in front of others. It is the clearest example for us that while we worship a God who is omnipotent and omniscient, we worship a God who understands what living this life is like. We worship a God who is "with us."

Are you sad today? Are you overjoyed? Are you hurting? Are you afraid? Regardless of your emotion, speak to God through it. Don't necessarily ask God to take the emotion away if that doesn't feel appropriate, but ask God to be there and to understand. Jesus is the best counselor you could imagine. He can be with you in your emotions, understand them, experience them, and engage with you in them. If you're happy, let God be happy with you. If you are sad, let God be sad with you. Find some solace in knowing that you are not alone. God is celebrating with you and weeping with you at all times.

# My Journal

...................................................................................
...................................................................................
...................................................................................
...................................................................................
...................................................................................
...................................................................................
...................................................................................
...................................................................................
...................................................................................
...................................................................................
...................................................................................
...................................................................................
...................................................................................
...................................................................................
...................................................................................
...................................................................................
...................................................................................
...................................................................................

# 10: Sunday Morning

*Lent Twenty-Five: Matthew 21:1-11; Isaiah 55:8-9*

Movies and television shows often have scenes where the hero makes a triumphant entrance to save the day. This is that point when the music swells, everyone stops and turns their heads, and people realize that the tide has turned. We live for that moment in our stories, because it gives us a sense of hope that the battle is never truly lost. Someone can always come in and save the day, and we can celebrate and cheer at his or her arrival. This is that moment for Jesus. Or rather, this is what the people believe is that moment for Jesus. They see Jesus as a revolutionary leader making his grand entrance into the city. They believe that he will lead an uprising over the religious and political leaders of the day. Yet Mariam and Salome seem to understand that things don't seem quite right. They've learned enough about Jesus to know that he is not doing things in the expected way. He is a man talking about peace and love and humility, rather than violence and fighting. Jesus is intentionally fulfilling the prophecy from Zechariah 9:9, and by doing so, he is claiming to be the long-awaited Messiah. These Israelites know their Scriptures, and they understand that this means their savior has arrived. Yet the way in which Jesus will truly fulfill all of these prophecies will be far different than what they expect. Where the Israelites don't have it quite right is that they think Jesus is going to be like William Wallace in Braveheart, when in reality Jesus is going to be more like, well, Jesus. As they come to the week of Passover, they are going to learn what a different kind of revolutionary Jesus actually is.

Do you ever wish Jesus was a little different? Perhaps you wish he would grant your wishes in life. Or perhaps you wish he would stage his second coming on your time schedule. The difficulty about following Jesus is seeing him for who he actually is. He is the Son of God, and his ways are "higher than your ways." His agenda was far greater than the agenda of the people who cheered him as he entered Jerusalem. In the same way, he asks that we see the world with an eternal perspective and operate differently as well. The world around you celebrates power, wealth, and influence. Contemplate how, today, you can have a higher agenda than the world's.

## *Lent Twenty-Six: Luke 6:46-49*

Most everyone has grown up with the story of the three little pigs, and we know that the life lesson is for us to take a little more time and to work with materials that are a little more substantial in order to have the strongest end result. The thing about this story is that its root is in this parable from Jesus. We know that we need a "firm foundation" when life's calamities come along. However, most people who preach on this passage will point out that Jesus makes an important distinction about the flood that comes, the *plēmmyra*. This term means an inevitable flood. There is no conditional "if." Jesus is telling us to prepare not for what might come our way, but for what will inevitably come our way. There will be hard seasons with tumultuous "weather," chaos, and heartache. But we're promised an opportunity to weather that storm if our foundation is built on God. For the three little pigs, you might ask, "If they knew for certain that the wolf would come knocking, wouldn't they have all taken the time to build their houses to be as strong as possible?" In Salome's conversation with the servant, Sarah, we see that the opportunity to build a strong house on a strong foundation is not reserved only for those with wealth or power but is open to everyone, a revolutionary idea in Jesus' day. The materials for building a strong relationship with God have been offered to everyone for free. All that is required is the willingness to be more like the third pig in the fairy tale, and less like the first two, to be willing to spend the time and effort in order to end up with a better result.

How would you grade your foundation today if you were inspecting it? You might say it's shifted or that it's not quite level. You might say it has a few cracks or that it has no real structure at all. Take some time to identify one thing you can do today, and then again tomorrow, and again the next day, that will offer you a stronger foundation in your relationship with God. Perhaps it's reading Scripture or reserving some dedicated time to pray before the start of your day. Put in the work today, because the storms and the wolves will come eventually, and God is calling us to be prepared.

## *Lent Twenty-Seven: Mark 11:15-19*

Salome and her family see a different side of Jesus today, a point that John Mark is happy to make. The peaceful Jesus displayed a moment of anger and frustration. The passage of Scripture where Jesus drives merchants out of the temple appears in each of the Gospels and serves as an important lesson about what the role of places of worship ought to be, but more importantly, about how we ought to treat others. The primary issue in this passage is not the idea that items were being sold in the temple, but that the items were being sold to exploit the poor and the widows in the community. In that time, it was the practice that the sacrifice of an animal needed to occur in order for the people to be restored to relationship with God. However, many people in the community did not have access to any animals for sacrifice, or if they did, it was often an "imperfect" specimen in the eyes of the religious leaders. During Passover, Israelites had gathered in Jerusalem from all over that area of the world, and merchants were attempting to take advantage of the situation financially by overcharging those who had nothing acceptable to sacrifice. Additionally, the money changers were set up in the temple to exchange currency at a significantly unfair rate to allow the poor and traveler to purchase needed sacrificial animals. They had turned what ought to have been a moment of holiness, love, and grace, a moment of receiving God's forgiveness freely, into one where people needed to pay money that they didn't have in order to receive God's forgiveness. This passage is less about whether a church has a bookstore near the entrance and more about what the church is doing in the community to care for those in need, and even more so, to not exploit them in that hour of need.

God has uniquely granted each of us the opportunity to serve and care for those around us. In your community, regardless of where you are, there are those in need and there are ministries and non-profits dedicated to providing for them. The encouragement today is to ask yourself how God has called you to serve those around you. The most consistent theme throughout Scripture, aside perhaps from the idea that God is working to save humanity from sin and brokenness, is the idea that humanity is called to care for others. Let us each live into that call today.

# My Journal

# 11 : Sunday Afternoon

*Lent Twenty-Eight: Isaiah 53; Matthew 16:13-16*

Have you ever seen the optical illusion in which the picture looks like a rabbit to some people and a duck to others? The lesson of the illusion is that the perspective from which people view the picture is incredibly important—it informs how they see it. The religious leaders of Jesus' time are growing restless. Jesus is this radical leader who has amassed a great following in a short amount of time. More importantly, nobody quite understands his end goal. From the perspective of his followers, the goal is to save them and overthrow Rome. From the perspective of the leaders in charge, the goal is a rebellion and chaos that will threaten the status quo. From these different perspectives, Jesus finds himself becoming more and more of a rebellious leader in the eyes of both parties. That is why he finds himself in the crosshairs of the Pharisees. However, neither side is actually listening to who Jesus says he is. They have all begun to see Jesus as what they want him to be or what they fear he is, and because of this, they are unable to see that Jesus is doing something grander than either side can imagine. Their confusion comes from an unwillingness to see the world the way God sees it—with the potential for redemption, love, and grace. In the end, he will neither overthrow an earthly government nor exclude the religious leaders from the promise of real, eternal life. He offers that even to them.

Is there someone around you with whom you often don't see eye-to-eye? When is the last time you made an effort to understand that person and his or her point of view without being judgmental or defensive? It is easier said than done, but imagine how you might view people if you saw them the way that Jesus sees them. They are loved and redeemed just as you are. Perhaps working to see things from their perspective will allow you to care for them in a new way.

# My Journal

# 12: Sunday Evening

*Lent Twenty-Nine: Matthew 21:28-32*

Stories are good for us. They encourage us, inspire us, and challenge us. Sometimes we avoid stories in favor of facts and figures, but a story is about people. Stories help us get to the heart of the matter. For this very reason, Jesus always taught with stories, with parables. Many times when someone tried to pin Jesus into a corner in a theological debate, Jesus would sidestep the conversation altogether and tell a story as his answer. What Jesus understood, and what we often miss, is that the people in the stories show us the heart of what God is trying to say. The heart of God's work on earth is, in fact, us. The people. Not the religious laws. Jesus' parables allow us to see that things aren't usually about black-and-white rules, but instead teach us about the best ways of living in community and relationship with one another. This doesn't mean there aren't rules. Of course there are. Murder is wrong, and we have a rule against murder. But underneath our rules lie the emotional and relational ramifications of murder that explain why it is wrong. The reason that Salome, her family, and everyone around them are drawn to Jesus is because his lessons are about people and about how God's will produces goodness in their lives.

In the parable of the two sons, one son said all of the right things. He outwardly behaved in an upstanding manner. But he didn't end up doing anything for his father at all. The other son had a rebellious heart, but in the end he repented. He turned around and went to work for his father. Jesus was calling out the religious leaders who were outwardly pious but were doing nothing to help the people around them. Is there a difference between saying all of the right things on the surface and actually getting down to doing the work of God?

# My Journal

# 13: Monday

*Lent Thirty: Luke 20:9-19*

Any time conversations begin about what is rightfully ours versus what is not ours, it is easy to become defensive. We want to reap what we've sowed. We want what is ours. It's a perfectly natural response. This attitude, however, flies in the face of a simple truth: all we've been given comes from God. We often say that we believe that, but then we behave as if we don't. Sometimes we confuse different ideas and think that if we have more, then we are more blessed, instead of realizing that we've been blessed with more, so that we can go forth and bless others more. What we have is not of our own making (who among us got to choose which country or which family we were born into?). Instead, the gifts, the talents, the resources that we have been given are ours to use for God's kingdom. What Salome finds in the tenant parable is that, while some rewards are the result of our work, what is given by God is given freely and not in response to any of us being better or more revered. The tenants of that story are just that: tenants. Renters. This world is not ours. God created this world and asked us to be stewards, caretakers. The hardest part of that truth is not even acknowledging that God has blessed us. The hardest part is knowing that those of us who have the "most" on this earth are the ones who are expected to do the most work of all!

What treasured possessions do you have? What have you been given that enabled you to be successful? Take a moment to listen to God and ask, "So because I've been given all of this, what am I to do with it? Should I give more to the church? Should I volunteer more of my time? Should I listen more to the people who are struggling?" Then, after you feel a nudge from God on your heart, go and do that thing.

## Lent Thirty-One: Mark 12:13-17

Nobody likes taxes. It's a simple truth. Everyone would be much happier without taxes. Yet here we find an important lesson from Jesus, which is to live as an upstanding member of society and to do what is right and necessary for the whole group to thrive. In this lesson, the church leaders are questioning Jesus in an attempt to trap him and find some basis to arrest him. These men were in charge of the Sanhedrin, which was the religious authority of the Israelites. Since the Israelites were also under Roman rule, they were subject to Roman laws and taxes. In questioning Jesus about these taxes, the pharisees were trying to pin Jesus down. Either Jesus says that Roman taxes are good and should be paid (thus making him unpopular with the Israelite people) or he tells the people not to pay their taxes (thus making him an enemy of the Roman Empire). Jesus, as usual, turns things around. Instead of choosing one of those options, he makes a distinction between worldly powers and the greater authority, which is God. He makes the point that it is not inherently wrong to abide by secular rules and pay your taxes. At the same time, he wants us to recognize that there is a greater authority than worldly governments. Give to God what is God's. We already know that everything belongs to God, but here, Jesus is not making that point. Jesus is demonstrating an understanding of earthly, political structures and our need to live within them. Scholars have come to claim that by paying taxes, Jesus was in fact teaching the people to live within their society as good citizens who strive to change corruption from within, rather than using violent rebellion.

You likely have areas in your life that you wish were different, legal structures and entities that you wish were different. The beauty of the message here is that Jesus does not dismiss working within the political and legal structures to evoke change for the kingdom of God. He condemns corruption and the abuse of power. Today, take some time to recognize the goodness of the structure around you and pray about how God might be calling you to be a voice of change for the parts of that structure that are no longer good. In all of this, remember that politics and societal structures are made up of people, and that Jesus would call upon you to treat everyone, regardless of position, with love and grace.

# My Journal

..................................................................................................
..................................................................................................
..................................................................................................
..................................................................................................
..................................................................................................
..................................................................................................
..................................................................................................
..................................................................................................
..................................................................................................
..................................................................................................
..................................................................................................
..................................................................................................
..................................................................................................
..................................................................................................
..................................................................................................
..................................................................................................
..................................................................................................
..................................................................................................
..................................................................................................

# 14: Wednesday

One of the most pivotal moments in the story of Jesus is when he emotionally turns toward the cross. During his early ministry, Jesus actively attempted to avoid being noticed for his works, because it wasn't time yet for the implications of his message to play out. But the truth is, his life and ministry were always going to lead to this end, and he understood that better than anyone. When the time came, he set his eyes upon Jerusalem, and accordingly, upon the cross. What we see with Salome in this part of the story is that the people are coming to the same realization: Jesus' actions can only lead to one place. The story only ends with Jesus' arrest. What he is preaching is too radical for the authorities to ignore. While you are incredibly unlikely in modern times to be arrested for being a Christian, specifically in this country, you can face ridicule and judgment for living your faith out in real ways. The question before you is, "Is it worth it?" There will be times when you might make someone uncomfortable, or you might have to forego something that you otherwise would want to do. People around you might look at you differently, leave you out of conversations, and choose to not invite you to gatherings. The hope of the gospel is that the life you live and the radical love and grace you extend is the only way to live. It is worth it! When we realize that we must emotionally turn and move toward the cross ourselves, we find the fullness of life that God saw for us when we were created.

Is fear of rejection preventing you from living out your faith in the way that you would like to be living it? Are you worried that truly living out your faith would change your life too much? Today, spend some time in prayer, asking God to motivate you to pursue that life. It is not easy, and it will mean change, which is scary. But it will be worth it. There is fulfillment and joy at the cross. Prepare yourself to move toward it.

# My Journal

.......................................................................................

.......................................................................................

.......................................................................................

.......................................................................................

.......................................................................................

.......................................................................................

.......................................................................................

.......................................................................................

.......................................................................................

.......................................................................................

.......................................................................................

.......................................................................................

.......................................................................................

.......................................................................................

.......................................................................................

.......................................................................................

.......................................................................................

.......................................................................................

# 15: Wednesday Evening

## *Lent Thirty-Three: Mark 14:12-31*

Passover is a tradition in the Jewish faith that stems from the Israelite people's time in Egypt as slaves. In an attempt to persuade Pharaoh to release the Israelites from bondage, God told Moses that all of the firstborn children in the region would die unless they marked their doorways, in which case the plague would "pass over" the household. Centuries later, Jesus and his disciples celebrate and remember this act of God to deliver their people. It is at this meal that Jesus gives one of his final lessons. He explains that a new covenant has been created between God and humanity. It is the final covenant and the one that extends to all people. In this covenant, Christ is the ultimate sacrifice, and through his spilt blood and broken body, we receive grace, forgiveness, and redemption.

While the disciples did not understand this concept as it was being taught, it came to form the very basis of the early church tradition. We see in the book of Acts that the early church was practicing communion as a way of remembering Jesus' sacrifice. Communion celebrates this moment in Scripture, and it is on Maundy (from the Latin mandatum, "command") Thursday during Holy Week, the days leading to Easter, that we remember that night and Jesus' "Last Supper" with his disciples. In communion, we partake in the covenant, experience forgiveness for our sins, and are strengthened for service. There are many different understandings of exactly what the elements of bread and wine/juice mean (if you're curious, Google transubstantiation, consubstantiation, and memorialism). What is apparent in all of it, however, is the idea that Jesus offers a gift in the form of those elements. Through those elements, we join the disciples in receiving divine grace at the table with Christ.

Begin to prepare yourself for Easter Sunday. It is Holy Week, and it is nearly time to experience the fullness of this climactic moment in the gospel story. In order to prepare yourself, make plans to attend a Maundy Thursday service this week. Partake in the elements. Confess the ways you have failed to love God and others. Receive forgiveness, enter into this New Covenant that God made with all of humanity, and leave knowing that you go forth with the Holy Spirit giving you strength and resolve for the path ahead.

# My Journal

# 16-18: Thursday Morning, Evening, and Night

*Lent Thirty-Four: Matthew 26:36-56*

The narrative of Jesus in the garden is one that is haunting, inspiring, and beautiful. (Remember, the character of John Mark is fictionalized in Salome's story as a way for Salome's family to learn firsthand about this pivotal moment in Jesus' story.) Details of Jesus' arrest are told in all four Gospels, but what we must understand about the garden narrative is the willingness of Jesus to let it happen. If you have never been to Israel, you need to know that the garden sits looking at the walls of Jerusalem. This is important because Jesus would have seen the torches of the men coming to arrest him long before they arrived. However, the other side of the garden looks at mountains and caves, specifically the Mount of Olives. He would have been able to turn around and flee into the wilderness and never be found if he had wanted to. The garden story is important because it emphasizes the choice God made. When Jesus prays and says, "Not my will but yours," shortly before his arrest, he is actively choosing to remain in the place where he will be handed over to pain and death. He knows what is coming. But he chooses to stay. Oftentimes in life, we are confronted with a difficult choice or situation. We would do anything for an escape. It's a helpful reminder to us that, in those moments in the Garden of Gethsemane, Jesus chose to stay, because doing so allowed him to love us. In situations where we pray for an escape, are we presented with an opportunity to love others by staying?

As you walk through Holy Week, recognize how hard it must have been for the disciples to watch Jesus be arrested. Jesus himself was human and was tempted to stop it from happening. Yet ask yourself why Jesus chose to stay for you, why he chose to go through the pain and humiliation of dying for you. What inspired him to stay in the garden for your benefit? Christ knew you and loved you even then. If you don't believe that you are worthy, challenge yourself to love yourself a little more. Recognize that Christ deemed you worthy enough to be arrested for. Give thanks to God today, because Jesus stayed for you.

# My Journal

# 19: Friday Early Morning

*Lent Thirty-Five: Mark 14:53-72*

Peter's denial of Jesus is typical of our human weakness surfacing in the face of adversity. Peter was accused of knowing Jesus, of being a disciple, of being in the garden with Jesus, and of cutting off someone's ear in his effort to protect Jesus. Put simply, he was accused of being a faithful follower of Christ. However, in a moment of fear, he denied this three times just as Jesus had predicted would be the case. There are two important lessons here. The first is that, even though we should strive to be people of integrity, when pushed into uncomfortable situations, we sometimes fail. Maybe we are ashamed to pray in a public setting. Maybe we downplay a church event we attended. Maybe we don't speak up when we hear others being denigrated. God brings grace and forgiveness into those situations. Accept it. Don't vilify yourself. Just strive to be better. The second lesson is that, despite Peter's fear and weakness, Jesus ultimately used him as the foundation of his church. God can take our weaknesses and transform us. Just as Jesus' story will not end in this moment of pain and heartache, it's not the end of the story for Peter either. Redemption is coming.

Give yourself grace today. Maybe there is some element of your past that you refuse to forgive yourself for. How can you receive grace from God if you aren't even willing to receive it from yourself? God has forgiven you. Take some time to pray to God. Give thanks for this grace and forgiveness. Accept it, and then offer that same grace to yourself.

# My Journal

................................................................................

................................................................................

................................................................................

................................................................................

................................................................................

................................................................................

................................................................................

................................................................................

................................................................................

................................................................................

................................................................................

................................................................................

................................................................................

................................................................................

................................................................................

................................................................................

................................................................................

................................................................................

................................................................................

# 20: Friday Midday

*Lent Thirty-Six: Matthew 27:45-56*

Jesus was put to death. He was arrested and convicted for the crime of claiming to be the king of the Jews and for claiming to be the Son of God. This is actually a verifiable fact. Two thousand years ago, there lived a man who was baptized by someone named John in the Jordan River, who taught lessons for several years that angered the Jewish authorities, who claimed to be God, who was arrested and killed for this, and whose followers claimed that he then rose from the dead. All of these statements are considered to be factual by any credible historian. We have as many primary sources which verify those facts as we do for facts about the life of Plato, for example. The question has never been about whether Jesus existed. The question is, "Did he actually rise from the dead and was he actually God incarnate?" That question is vital. If God entered into humanity and intentionally died for us, that means that God is with us until the end. In our darkest moments, in our final breaths, in our tears and pain and worst days, God is with us. Because God remained on the cross until he died, God experienced the worst that the world had to give and now remains with us no matter how bad it gets around us. The name *Emmanuel*, literally translated "God with us," is manifested by this moment on the cross. This is the moment Holy Week has been pushing us toward, this pain and sadness and grief. Yet, there is hope on Good Friday. Hope comes from the fact that God stayed with us. The Jewish people believed that the veil in the temple separated the presence of God from the people. The day of Jesus' death, it was torn open, and all separation between heaven and earth, between God and humanity, was also torn away. God is forever with us from our highest highs to our lowest lows. Today we celebrate, and today we mourn. God is still with us.

Reflect in silence on the chilling and comforting truth that God has never left us. No matter what you do or what you say, God has not and will not leave you. Regardless of the pain and heartache you cause, God has not and will not leave you. Let this truth push you forward as you celebrate the wonder of Good Friday. A day of death and sadness will not defeat us, because God has not and will not leave us.

# My Journal

# 21: Friday Evening

*Lent Thirty-Seven: Matthew 27:57-66*

The moments between Good Friday and Easter morning are confusing and difficult. We know how the story ends. We've seen the movies and read the Scriptures. We know Jesus will rise again. Yet Salome's story helps us see where the disciples and the followers of Christ would have been in this moment. They had left their jobs and their families behind. They had been following him for three years and had certainly been betting on the promise of Jesus' revolution. He was supposed to fix everything. Now they were grappling with a burial and the possibility that Jesus was a fraud. At that point in time, they had every reason to believe that he was a fraud. He could not be their expected Messiah, certainly not the Son of God. He must have been simply another prophet who had been killed for his teachings. This "in-between moment" for the disciples is helpful for us, because it is where we often find ourselves. We believe that God has conquered death and that eternal life is coming, but we are still stuck in limbo in this earthly life with all of its hardships and heartaches. The hope of the gospel is believing that God is at work in God's time and that the world continues to move forward because God is reconciling everything back to God. As the old saying goes, "If it is not well in the end, it is not yet the end."

Take some time to reflect today on your worst moments, and then take some time to reflect on how you got from those moments to where you are today. Can you remember times when it was hard to believe that everything would turn out okay? In retrospect, how was God present in bringing you back to a place of joy and glory each step of the way? As you hold vigil for Jesus in the wake of his death, remind yourself that this vigil doesn't last forever. The promise of tomorrow cannot be undone.

# My Journal

# 22-23: Saturday and Sunday

*Lent Thirty-Eight: Luke 24:1-12*

"Christ is risen." "He is risen indeed." This call and response has been the rallying cry for Christians since Jesus reentered the world. Like a collegiate chant that ties students and alumni to their university, "He is risen indeed" is the affirming call that the truth of Christ is alive and well for us. Note the present tense of the verb. Christ didn't live a little while longer and then eventually die again. Christ rose from the grave and never died again. He conquered death. Christ lives today, and we are Easter people who celebrate this promise. It's hard to contemplate what this means for our lives today. Honestly, it sounds unbelievable. Men don't come back from the dead. They certainly shouldn't be able to move massive boulders blocking their exit or walk past armed guards. As unbelievable as it sounds, Christ rose from the grave. This truth should inform every action we take for the rest of our lives! We ought to talk to people differently because Christ is risen. We ought to make different decisions at work because Christ is risen. We ought to love people more abundantly because Christ is risen. We now live in a world where we do not need to fear death. We get to live lives of joy and hope because death has been defeated and we confidently claim the promise of life after death, real life where we are joined with God forever. How can our lives ever be the same?

Sing praises to God today, for Jesus Christ is risen. He has conquered death and made a new life for you. There is a promise of tomorrow and a hope that is everlasting. In the middle of Easter eggs, pastel-colored dresses, and cute bow ties on toddlers, celebrate the risen Lord and the joy we find in him. Live differently today with greater joy and hope and love for the world around you. Carry that into tomorrow and the next day. The work of Easter only begins on Easter Sunday. It continues every day from this day forward.

# My Journal

# 24: Sometime Later

*Lent Thirty-Nine: Luke 24:13-49*

How do you end a story well? The story of Salome ends with a letter from her cousin Mariam. The story of Jesus' life on earth ends with an empty tomb. Although each of the Gospels includes slightly different details, they all end with an empty tomb. Everything about that feels impossible. Humans do not come back to life. Yet, the entire truth of God's redemption hinges on that reality! Right after Jesus' resurrection, he appeared to several of his disciples, including the two on the road to Emmaus, to many of the disciples in the upper room and to doubting Thomas. They are not condemned for at first doubting what has happened. They are given opportunities to experience the truth for themselves. Each disciple is confronted with the truth that the world was forever changed by the greatest of miracles. While it may seem like a fable or a massive conspiracy, it's important to remember that over 500 people saw Jesus after he rose from the dead and many of them would have still been alive when the Gospels were written. We have more primary source evidence for Jesus' resurrection than we do for the actions of many people in history. Yet, we have a hard time truly accepting the miracle of the fact that God entered human history, was crucified for each of us and then absolutely, really, rose from the dead. We say we believe that, but do we fully comprehend it?

Today, take the time to sit with that truth. The implications of the fact that the God of the universe is alive, and loves each one of us, should turn our world upside down. Do you every doubt the possibility? If so, ask God to engage with you so that you too can experience the same truth as Thomas and so many others. If you truly believe that Jesus rose from the dead, what implication does that have for your life?

## *Lent Forty: Matthew 28:16-20*

Matthew ends with the Great Commission, the command to go and baptize others in the name of Christ and to spread the gospel narrative to others. Telling others about Jesus is terrifying and difficult. We risk our social capital if we go out on a limb for anything, much less something as controversial as religion, What if we upset other people? What if their experience with church isn't as powerful as ours? What if we say something wrong? What if they don't believe us or think we're crazy? All of these are valid concerns, but none of them preclude you from speaking about your faith. You don't have to have all of the facts exactly right. It's not even your responsibility to ensure that their church experience and their relationship with Jesus is like yours. Just share your personal experience with Jesus and leave the rest up to God.

Even though the Gospels have an ending, the story of Christ doesn't. That story is still being written, and we are the latest characters in it! The story of Christ continues through our words and our deeds. You are living out the story of Christ to this day through your life and your loving. The question for us is not whether the story is good enough to share. The question is how we're going to carry the story forward ourselves, like generations have before us.

Future generations will also carry the good news forward after we are gone – if we share it today.

Go forth, spread the gospel, and continue the story. . . .

# My Journal

........................................................................................
........................................................................................
........................................................................................
........................................................................................
........................................................................................
........................................................................................
........................................................................................
........................................................................................
........................................................................................
........................................................................................
........................................................................................
........................................................................................
........................................................................................
........................................................................................
........................................................................................
........................................................................................
........................................................................................
........................................................................................
........................................................................................

www.ingramcontent.com/pod-product-compliance
Lightning Source LLC
Chambersburg PA
CBHW071154120626
46546CB00006B/2256